Printed in China

CCTV

快乐中国——学汉语
Happy China – Learning Chinese

中国中央电视台
《快乐中国——学汉语》栏目组 编

杭州

篇

北京语言大学出版社

杭州

杭州主要景点游览示意图

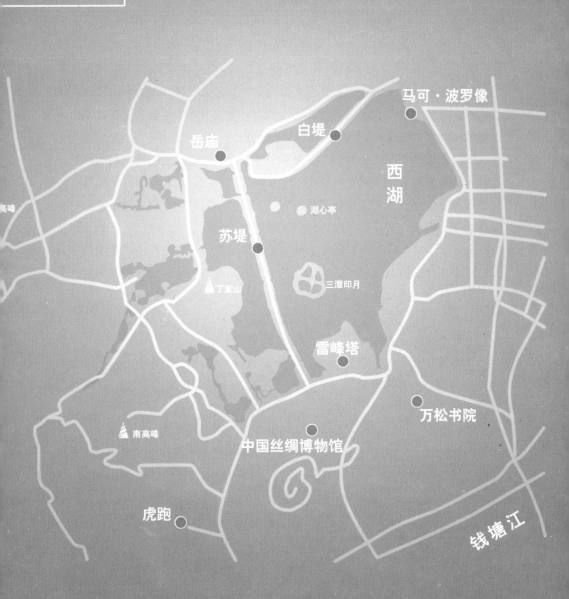

马可·波罗像

白堤

岳庙

西湖

湖心亭

苏堤

丁家山

三潭印月

雷峰塔

南高峰

万松书院

中国丝绸博物馆

虎跑

钱塘江

前　言

中国的发展令世人瞩目，随之而来的学汉语热潮也在全球兴起。

中国中央电视台中文国际频道（CCTV-4）《快乐中国——学汉语》栏目，与中国各地城市以及风景名胜点合作，把饱览名山大川、感受中华民族历史文化与学习汉语结合起来，将汉语言语技能与知识性、趣味性和欣赏性融为一体，创办了独特的寓教于乐的电视教学节目——《快乐中国——学汉语》。

通过中央电视台覆盖全球98%的强势传媒，《快乐中国——学汉语》自2004年6月播出以来，引起了海内外观众的热烈反响。不少观众来信来电，希望得到《快乐中国——学汉语》栏目播出节目的文字和音像材料，作为学习汉语的视听说教材。为了满足广大观众的需要，北京语言大学出版社承担了这套文字、声像教材的编辑、出版任务。在此，我们深表感谢！

语言是桥梁，电视是桥梁，《快乐中国——学汉语》是沟通你我的桥梁。它把汉语教学搬进大自然的课堂之中，"快乐学汉语，轻松又好记！"此外，我们采用高清晰电视技术和立体声制作的表现手段，并制作成可用于教学的、有多种字幕选择的DVD，充分展示汉语特有的魅力。

为了使节目主持人的对话更好地帮助您学说汉语，我们聘请了北京语言大学长期从事对外汉语教学和英语教学的几位教授，对每一集对话进行了加工，增添了生词、注释、替换练习和会话等部分，并负责生词和注释部分的英文翻译。每一集有8～10个生词，有5～8个注释，有模仿练习，也有交际性的活用练习，帮助您更好地理解对话内容，掌握重点词句。

为了适应学习者需要，每册收入15集节目（特殊情况除外），并配有相应拍摄点的简介、图片和旅游资讯。由于节目制作还在进行之中，配套图书将陆续出版。

中国中央电视台中文国际频道

《快乐中国——学汉语》栏目组

PREFACE

The development of China has attracted the attention of the world, as a result of which a great upsurge for learning Chinese has been going on throughout the world.

The CCTV-4 program *Happy China—Learning Chinese* offers learners an opportunity to learn the Chinese language and culture while enjoying the beautiful scenic spots in China. Co-operating with the local administrations of the well-known scenic spots, this program well combines the learning of language skills with that of Chinese culture and history in an interesting, informative and enjoyable way.

With a 98% coverage in the world, the program of CCTV was broadcast since June, 2004. Quite a lot of the viewers expressed the hope to have the language materials as a learning aid. In view of this, we have invited Beijing Language and Culture University Press, a leading press in publications on Chinese learning materials for foreigners, to produce and publish these language materials for our viewers.

Apart from the language materials presented in the program, Words and Expressions, Notes, Substitution Drills and Conversations are provided in each book, among which Words and Expressions and Notes are accompanied with brief English translations or explanations. Each book is composed of about 15 episodes of the TV program with brief introductions and photos of corresponding scenic spots and travel guides. As more episodes of *Happy China—Learning Chinese* are coming up, more books will be published accordingly.

CCTV-4

Happy China—Learning Chinese Production Team

杭 州

杭州，浙江省省会，一个闻名中外的旅游城市。它位于中国的东南沿海、钱塘江下游北岸，距离上海仅151公里。杭州拥有2,200多年的悠久历史，是中国的七大古都之一，曾是吴越国和南宋王朝的建都之地。

独特的自然环境和深厚的历史底蕴，使得杭州拥有众多自然景观和人文景观。杭州有两个国家级风景名胜区——西湖风景名胜区和富春江-新安江-千岛湖风景名胜区，同时还拥有14个国家重点文物保护单位和3个国家级博物馆。世界上最长的人工运河——京杭大运河也南起杭州。13世纪意大利旅行家马可·波罗曾盛赞杭州是"世界上最美丽的华贵之城"。

本书介绍的主要景点有西湖、保俶塔、六和塔、岳庙、万松书院等。另外，还介绍了杭州有名的丝绸、茶叶、工艺品和美食。

俗话说"上有天堂，下有苏杭"，天堂般的美景每年都吸引着成千上万的国内外游客来到西子湖畔，享受那平静的湖水、幽美的园林、古老的寺庙、雅致的茶馆……

An Introduction of Hangzhou

Hangzhou, the capital of Zhejiang Province, is a well-known tourist city at home and abroad.

Located on the southeastern coast of China, northern bank of the lower reaches of Qiantang River, it is 151 kilometers from Shanghai. With a history of over 2,200 years, Hangzhou is one of the seven Chinese ancient capitals. It was once the capital of the Kingdom of Wuyue during the Five Dynasties and the Southern Song Dynasty.

Endowed with unique natural environment and a culture of thousands of years, Hangzhou has lots of scenic spots. There are two national scenic areas in Hangzhou: the West Lake Scenic Area and the Fuchun River-Xin'an River-Qiandao Lake Scenic Area. Hangzhou is also the southern end of the Beijing-Hangzhou Grand Canal, the longest canal in the world. In addition there are 14 national cultural relics and 3 national museums in Hangzhou. In the 13th century, an Italian traveler Marco Polo admired Hangzhou as "the most beautiful and splendid city in the world".

The major tourist attractions include the West Lake, Liuhe Pagoda, Baochu Pagoda, and Yue Fei Temple, Wansong Academy, etc. Hangzhou is also famous for its silk, tea, handicrafts and delicacies.

As a popular saying goes: "Above in the sky there is heaven, while down on earth there are Hangzhou and Suzhou." Each year, Hangzhou's heavenly beauty attracts tens of thousands of tourists to the exquisite West Lake to enjoy the placid lake, beautiful gardens, antique temples and elegant teahouses…

目录
CONTENTS

杭州

【第一集】

西湖畔马可·波罗像

大　牛：快乐的大牛，在美丽的杭州向您问好！从今天开始，我们就
　　　　要快快乐乐游杭州。这么迷人的西湖啊！我们当然要请出一
　　　　位神秘的嘉宾。她是当地人，而且我听说她是一位美女①。

韩　佳：大牛，欢迎你来杭州啊。

大　牛：韩佳，你来了！但是还有一位神秘的当地的嘉宾，她在哪
　　　　儿啊？

韩　佳：远在天边，近在眼前。

大　牛：啊，就是你啊！

韩　佳：对呀，我就是从小在西湖边长大的杭州人。

大　牛：哦，原来是这样。马可·波罗称赞杭州是世界上最美丽的华
　　　　贵之城。我可要好好逛逛你的家乡。

韩　佳：好啊！马可·波罗称赞杭州是世界上最美丽的华贵之城。

Hángzhōu shì shìjiè shàng zuì měilì de huáguì zhī chéng.
杭州 是世界 上 最美丽 的 华贵 之 城。

Hangzhou is the most beautiful and splendid city in the world.

Daniel: I am happy Daniel, saying hello to you from the beautiful Hangzhou. From now on, we will enjoy a tour in Hangzhou. How charming the West Lake is! We will certainly invite a mysterious guest to our program. She is a native of Hangzhou. Besides, it is said that she is a beauty.

Han Jia: Daniel, welcome to Hangzhou.

Daniel: Han Jia, here you are. But we have a mysterious native guest. Where is she?

Han Jia: She is right in front of your eyes.

Daniel: Wow, so it is you.

Han Jia: Right. I am from Hangzhou. I grew up by the West Lake.

Daniel: Oh, so it is. Marco Polo once said that Hangzhou is the most beautiful and splendid city in the world. I will have a great tour in your hometown.

Han Jia: All right. Marco Polo commended Hangzhou as the most beautiful and gorgeous city in the world.

场景 Scene　杭州街上

韩　佳："未曾抛得杭州去，一半勾留是此湖。"哎，大牛，游杭州啊，
　　　最先应该游的就是西湖。

大　牛：没错，说到杭州的美景，西湖可是杭州的一颗明珠。我们就
　　　从那儿出发吧。

韩　佳：OK。杭州是先有水，再有城。那么西湖是先有堤，再有岛。
　　　所以我们最先应该去看看有名的苏堤。

大　牛：好吧，走！

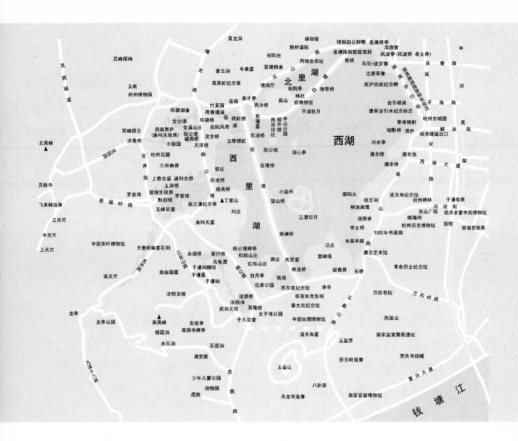

Han Jia: Can't fully withdraw from Hangzhou, half of the memory is lingering at the West Lake. Hey, Daniel, when you travel in Hangzhou, the first place you should visit is the West Lake.

Daniel: Exactly. I heard that when talking about Hangzhou's scenery, the West Lake is the pearl on the crown. We should start there.

Han Jia: OK. Hangzhou had lakes first and city afterwards. Well, the West Lake had causeways first and islets afterwards. We should go and visit the famous Su Causeway first.

Daniel: OK. Let's go.

韩　佳：大牛，现在我们在的这个地方，就是苏堤。这条堤就是苏东坡在当官的时候筑下的，它贯通了西湖的南北。后人为了纪念苏东坡对西湖作出的巨大贡献，所以就把这条堤命名为"苏公堤"，简称"苏堤"。

大　牛：你看，苏堤的两边，一棵桃树、一棵柳树，都是这样种的。

韩　佳：对呀，所以到了春天，苏堤春晓，桃红柳绿，才得了"西湖十景"之一的美称啊！

大　牛：苏堤春晓，"春"就是"春天"的"春"。

韩　佳：对。

大　牛：那"晓"是什么意思呢？

韩　佳："晓"就是指天刚刚亮。春天清晨的苏堤可美极了②。

大　牛：你说得这么好，到底是不是这么美，我们也看不见呀！你可是跟我说过③，"耳听为虚，眼见为实"哦。

韩　佳：这个成语你用得倒挺是地方④。

大　牛：当然了！学会了就得会用嘛！

韩　佳：你看，我早有准备。

Wǒ zǎo yǒu zhǔnbèi.

我　早　有　准备。

I was prepared long ago.

6

Han Jia: Daniel, we are now at Su Causeway. It was built when Su Dongpo served as a government official here. It runs through the West Lake from the south to the north. In order to commemorate Su Dongpo's great contribution to the West Lake, people named this causeway as Sugong Causeway, and it was called Su Causeway for short.

Daniel: Look, on both sides of Su Causeway, peach trees and willows are interplanted.

Han Jia: Right. So in spring we have, Spring Dawn at Su Causeway, with red peach flowers and green willows. That's why it is listed as one of the ten famous views of the West Lake.

Daniel: In "su di chun xiao", "chun" means spring.

Han Jia: Right.

Daniel: Then what does "xiao" mean?

Han Jia: "Xiao" means dawn. Su Causeway at dawn in spring looks great.

Daniel: You said it was great, but we can't see whether it is really great or not. You once told me that "er ting wei xu, yan jian wei shi".

Han Jia: You used this idiom at the opportune place.

Daniel: Of course. We need to know how to use it once we learn it.

Han Jia: Look, I have made preparation in advance.

大　牛：红红绿绿的，还真是挺好看的。春天的时候，我一定再来亲眼看看苏堤春晓。

韩　佳：好了，西湖上还有另外一条堤呢！咱们也别走着看了⑤，换一种方式吧。走！

大　牛：又有什么新鲜玩意儿？去瞧瞧！

场景 Scene　白 堤

韩　佳：哎，大牛，咱们眼前的这条堤就叫"白堤"。

大　牛：哦，我知道了。苏堤就是苏东坡修筑的，这白堤自然就是白居易修筑的了？

韩　佳：错了吧！

大　牛：啊？

韩　佳：这白居易的确修过一条白公堤，不过不是这一条。这条白堤又叫"白沙堤"，在白居易修堤之前就已经有了。

大　牛：哦，原来是这样。

Daniel: Red and green. They are really wonderful. When spring comes again, I will certainly come to see Spring Dawn at Su Causeway.

Han Jia: All right. There is another causeway in the West Lake. Let's stop walking around and change to another way to do the sightseeing. Come on.

Daniel: Do you have anything novel? Let's go and take a look.

Han Jia: Hey, Daniel, the causeway in front of us is called Bai Causeway.

Daniel: Oh, I see. The Su Causeway was built by Su Dongpo. Bai Causeway must have been built by Bai Juyi.

Han Jia: You are wrong.

Daniel: What?

Han Jia: Bai Juyi did build a Baigong Causeway, but it was not this one. Bai Causeway is called Baisha Causeway as well. It was built before Bai Juyi built Baigong Causeway.

Daniel: I see.

画 舫

大　牛：韩佳，这才真叫游西湖啊。你看，船在湖中行，人在画中游。

韩　佳：哟，说得还挺好。这西湖上有三座岛，都是用湖中的泥堆积起来的人工岛屿。最小的那一座叫阮公墩，最大的那一座叫三潭印月。岛中有湖，湖中有岛。岛上的景色，美不胜收。

Dǎo shàng de jǐngsè měi bú shèng shōu.
岛　上　的 景色 美 不 胜　收。

There is lots of wonderful scenery on the island.

亭 子

大　牛：哎，韩佳，你看，那座塔细细高高的，好像很特别啊。

韩　佳：那就是宝俶塔，是西湖边上最为醒目的标志性建筑。

大　牛：哦，这么细的塔，好像人要是稍微胖了一点儿，就上不去了⑥。

韩　佳：胖的、瘦的都上不去，因为这座塔是实心的。

大　牛：什么叫"实心的"呀？

韩　佳："实心的"就是说这座塔的内部完全被填满了，没有一点空隙。

大　牛：哦，怪不得没人能爬上去呢⑦，因为它是实心的。

韩　佳：哎，这西湖边上还有另外一座塔呢！

大　牛：哦，在哪儿啊？

韩　佳：别找了，咱们过几天有机会去看看。

大　牛：她还不告诉我们呢！好，我们到"赏心悦目"里面去找找吧！

Daniel: Han Jia, this is called the West Lake cruise. Look, the boat is sailing on the lake and the visitors are like wandering in a painting.

Han Jia: Hey, wonderfully put. There are three islets in the West Lake. All of them were made by people using mud in the lake. The smallest one is called Ruangong Dun. The largest one is called Three Pools Mirroring the Moon. There are lakes on the islets and there are islets in the lakes. There are so many beautiful views on the islets that you simply can't take them all in.

Daniel: Hey, Han Jia, look at the slim and tall tower. It looks very unique.

Han Jia: That's Baochu Pagoda. It is the most eye-catching building by the West Lake.

Daniel: Hey, the pagoda is so slim that it seems that if people are chubbier, they won't be able to get up.

Han Jia: Neither the slim nor the chubby can go up there, because the pagoda is solid inside.

Daniel: What does "shixin de" mean?

Han Jia: "Shixin de" means that the inside of the tower is filled up and there is no space left.

Daniel: Oh. It's no wonder that no one can go up the tower because it's completely solid.

Han Jia: Hey, there is another pagoda by the West Lake.

Daniel: Well, where is it?

Han Jia: No need to look for it. We will take a look at it in a couple of days.

Daniel: She won't tell us. OK. Let's go to the Feast for the Eyes to look for it.

生词 Words and Expressions

1. 神秘 （形） shénmì mysterious
2. 嘉宾 （名） jiābīn honoured guests
3. 称赞 （动） chēngzàn to praise
4. 华贵 （形） huáguì luxurious
5. 明珠 （名） míngzhū jewel, bright pearl
6. 堤 （名） dī dyke, causeway
7. 贡献 （动、名） gòngxiàn to make contribution, contribution
8. 景色 （名） jǐngsè scenery
9. 美不胜收 měi bú shèng shōu more beauty than one can take in
10. 怪不得 （副） guàibude no wonder

注释 Notes

1. 她是当地人，**而且**我听说她是一位美女。

"而且"，连词，表示进一步的意思，前面常有"不仅、不但"跟它相呼应。

"而且"，a conjunction, is similar to "what's more". It is usually echoed by "不仅"，"不但" in the former sentence.

例如：他不仅英语好，而且法语说得也不错。

2. 春天清晨的苏堤**可**美极了。

"可"，副词，表示强调。

"可"，an adverb, is used for emphasis.

例如：山上的景色可好看了。

"形容词＋极＋了"这一结构表示程度最高，常用于口语。

"Adjective ＋ 极 ＋ 了 "，indicating the superlative degree, is used in spoken Chinese.

例如：今天来西湖游览的人多极了。

3. 你可是跟我说**过**……

这里"过"是动态助词，用在动词或少数形容词之后，表示过去曾经有过某种经历。

"过"，an dynamic auxiliary word，is used after a verb or a few adjectives to express the idea that something has happened or been done.

基本句式为：

The basic pattern is:

主语——谓语动词／形容词——过——宾语

Subject—predicate verb/adjective—过—object

你　　　　　说　　　　过。

我　　　　　见　　　　过　这个人。

否定式用"没有"。

The negative form is constructed by using"没有".

例如：我以前没有吃过饺子。

4. 这个成语你用得倒挺是地方。

"倒"，副词，这里用于舒缓语气，不用"倒"，语气较强。

"倒"，an adverb，is used here to soften the tone，and without it the tone would be harsher.

例如：有机会出去玩儿玩儿，倒也不错。

5. 咱们也别走着看了……

"着"，动态助词，表示一个动作或状态正在持续。

"着"，an auxiliary word，is used to show an action or a state is continuing.

基本句式为：

Its basic pattern is:

主语——谓语动词——着——宾语

Subject—predicate verb—着—object

学生们　　都坐　　　着。

他　　　穿　　　着　一件新毛衣。

"动词＋着"可以做状语，表示行为的方式。

"Verb + 着" can be used as an adverbial of manner.

例如：老师站着上课。

6. 好像人要是稍微胖了一点就上不去了。

这是一个假设复句，"要是"提出一种假设，"就"引出在这种情况会出现的结果。

"要是" is similar to "if...", and "就" (then) leads to the result.

例如：要是明天不下雨，我们去颐和园玩儿吧。

7. 怪不得没人能爬上去呢。

"怪不得"，副词，表示明白了原因，对某种情况就不感到奇怪。

"怪不得"，an adverb，is similar to "no wonder"。

例如：小王病了，怪不得他今天没来上课。

替换练习 Substitution Drills

1.	杭州	是世界上最	美丽	的	华贵之城。
	北京		古老		文化之城
	苏州		著名		丝绸之城
	广州		繁华		美食之城

2.	我早有	准备。
		感觉
		预防
		警惕

3.	岛	上的	景色	美不胜收。
	湖		风光	
	山		风景	
	展览会		工艺品	

14

会话　Conversations

完成下列会话 Complete the following dialogues
（如括号里有词语或提示，请按要求做 Use words or expressions given in the brackets）

A：西湖的景色怎么样？

B：太迷人了！你对西湖怎么这么熟悉？

A：我是杭州人啊。

B：＿＿＿＿＿＿＿＿＿＿＿＿＿＿＿＿＿＿＿。（怪不得）

· ·

A：听说西湖有几个有名的堤，是吗？

B：＿＿＿＿＿＿＿＿＿＿＿＿＿＿＿＿＿＿＿。（不仅……而且……）

A：西湖有几个岛？你能介绍一下吗？

B：好。

杭州

【第二集】

场景 Scene 杭州街上

大　牛：哎，韩佳，我发现你今天穿的衣服特别好看。

韩　佳：是吗？谢谢！

大　牛：而且你们看，她的妆化得真不错①。

韩　佳：大牛，你是不是又有什么事儿想求我啊？

大　牛：其实，韩佳，是这样的，我在杭州人生地不熟的，全靠你了。

韩　佳：没问题，你是我的搭档，我总不能抛下你不管吧。放心吧，
　　　　　我啊，一定当好你的向导，接着带你逛西湖。走吧！

大　牛：中国那句俗话说得真不错，"在家靠父母，出门靠朋友。"

Zài jiā kào fùmǔ, chū mén kào péngyou.
在　家　靠　父母，　出　门　靠　朋友。

When at home people rely on their parents, when away they rely on friends.

Daniel: Hey, Han Jia, I found that you are wonderfully dressed today.

Han Jia: Really? Thank you.

Daniel: Look, she's got nice makeup too.

Han Jia: Daniel, what are you up to? Are you asking me for something?

Daniel: Actually, Han Jia, you know, I am not familiar with Hangzhou, so I totally depend on you.

Han Jia: No problem. You are my partner, so I can't leave you alone. Don't worry. I will be a good tour guide. I am going to show you around the West Lake. Let's go.

Daniel: That old Chinese saying is right. "When at home people rely on their parents, when away they rely on friends."

黄龙洞投缘池

大　牛：哎，韩佳。

韩　佳：嗯？

大　牛：你这是在干吗呢？

韩　佳：哎，大牛，这里是投缘石。哎，你看，地上的那些分别代表姻缘、财缘，还有文缘。你呀，选择其中的一个位置，站在上面向中间投币，看你能不能投中②。

大　牛：哦，这个有意思。我来试试，看我大牛能不能发财。完了，看来我大牛这一辈子都得过苦日子了！

韩　佳：行啦，你还当真啊！这只不过是一种游戏。哎，你再去那里试试！

大　牛：啊，"文"，韩佳，你就别老让我读书了吧③！

韩　佳：嗨，你就试试吧！

大　牛：投中了！我大牛天生就是读书的料，没办法，没办法！

韩　佳：他还来劲了！

Daniel: Hey, Han Jia.

Han Jia: Yes?

Daniel: What are you doing?

Han Jia: Hey, Daniel, it is Tou Yuan Stone. Hey, look, the things on the ground represent marriage, fortune and academic achievements. Choose one of these spots, stand on it and toss a coin to the center and see if you can make it.

Daniel: Well, this is fun. Let me try and see if I can make a fortune. Bad luck, it seems I will have to lead a hard life.

Han Jia: Forget about it. Don't take it seriously. It's only a game. Hey, go there and have a try.

Daniel: Wow, academic achievements, Han Jia, don't let me keep on studying.

Han Jia: Hey, just have a try.

Daniel: I got it. I was born a bookworm. That's my fate, my fate.

Han Jia: He is taking it seriously.

大　牛：哎，韩佳，你看，这里有那么多条鱼！你看那条鱼多肥呀！
　　　　它吃什么好吃的了？

韩　佳：哎呀，你看这些红鲤鱼把湖水都染成红色了。哎，大牛，那
　　　　边有一条鱼朝你游过来了，赶紧给它准备美食！

大　牛：好。哎呀，这些鱼哪儿是在吃食，简直就是在抢食儿④！

韩　佳：花港的鱼真是太幸福了！

Huāgǎng de yú zhēn shì tài xìngfú le!
花港 的 鱼 真 是 太 幸福 了!

The fish at Huagang are very lucky.

Daniel: Hey, Han Jia, look. There are lots of fish here. Look, that fish is so plump. What does it eat?

Han Jia: Hey, look at these red carps. They dye the lake red. Hey, Daniel, a fish is coming your way. Feed it quickly.

Daniel: All right. Wow, these fish are not eating. They are actually fighting for food.

Han Jia: The fish at the Flower Harbor are very lucky.

杭
州

柳浪闻莺处

韩　佳：哎，大牛，你知道吗？这西湖的景观不光有视觉上的，还有
　　　　听觉上的呢。

大　牛：听觉上的，怎么讲？

韩　佳：你看，这沿岸种了500多棵柳树。清风吹来，柳条就像绿色
　　　　的波涛一样翻滚起来。

大　牛：可是柳树跟听觉又有什么关系呀⑤？

韩　佳：嘘，你仔细听！

大　牛：哦，有小鸟的叫声。

韩　佳：嗯，没错，这就是著名的西湖又一景——柳浪闻莺。

大　牛：这里的"闻"是二声，不是用鼻子闻，是"听"的意思。

韩　佳：嗯，没错。哎，大牛，这西湖上还有一景，也和听觉有关。

大　牛：啊，还有一景是什么？

韩　佳："南屏晚钟"，你听！

Han Jia: Hey, Daniel, do you know that the West Lake has not only visual views, but also auditory views?

Daniel: What do you mean?

Han Jia: Look, more than 500 willows are planted on the banks. When breeze blows, the twigs of the willows roll like green waves.

Daniel: But do willows have anything to do with the sense of hearing?

Han Jia: Listen carefully.

Daniel: Well, birds are chirping.

Han Jia: Right. It is another famous view of West Lake, Listening to Orioles Singing in the Willows.

Daniel: Note that, "wen" here with the second tone, doesn't mean to smell, but means to listen or to hear.

Han Jia: Right. Hey, Daniel, there is another view of the West Lake that is related to the sense of hearing.

Daniel: Well, what is it?

Han Jia: Evening Bell Ringing at Nanping Hill. Listen.

南屏晚钟处

韩　佳：怎么样？大牛，这声音够响亮的吧！

大　牛：啊，什么？

韩　佳：我说这声音够宏亮的吧！

大　牛：够宏亮的！

韩　佳：那当然。这个钟声一响起来，半个杭州城都能听见。

大　牛：那我也来敲一敲。现在轮到我大牛了！

　　　　一祝大牛学习进步！

　　　　二祝韩佳学习进步！

　　　　三祝《快乐中国》所有的观众朋友们学习进步！

Zhù　péngyoumen　xuéxí　jìnbù !
祝　　朋友们　　学习　进步 !

We hope that all our friends make good progress in their studies!

Han Jia: How is that? Daniel, is it resounding enough?

Daniel: Wow, sorry?

Han Jia: Is the bell resounding?

Daniel: Yes.

Han Jia: Of course. Once the bell rings, half of Hangzhou can hear it.

Daniel: I am going to ring the bell. It's my turn.

May Daniel make progress in his study.

May Han Jia make progress in her study.

May all the viewers of Happy China make progress in their studies.

平湖秋月

韩　佳：大牛，这里就是西湖上赏月最好的地方了。当年康熙皇帝来
　　　　到这里看过之后，留下了"平湖秋月"四个字。

大　牛："平湖秋月"，现在正是秋天，平静的湖水、秋天的月亮，我
　　　　们来的正是时候。

韩　佳：是啊，"一色湖光万顷秋"。

大　牛：嗯，我们今天看过的美景可真是不少。怪不得人们常说：
　　　　"上有天堂，下有苏杭"，果然不假⑥。

韩　佳：下面就让我们再到"赏心悦目"里，去欣赏一下西湖的美景吧！

Han Jia: Daniel, this is the best place to view the moon at the West Lake. When Emperor Kangxi came and saw the moon here, he left four characters "Ping Hu Qiu Yue".

Daniel: The Autumn Moon over the Calm Lake. Now it is autumn. The calm lake and the autumn moon. We came at the opportune time.

Han Jia: Right. The calm lake gives you a glimpse of all the beauty of autumn.

Daniel: Right. We saw a lot of beautiful scenery today. No wonder people often say "Just as there is a paradise in heaven, there are Suzhou and Hangzhou on earth". It is true.

Han Jia: Let's go to the Feast for the Eyes again to enjoy the marvelous scenery of the West Lake.

生词　Words and Expressions

1.	化妆		huà zhuāng	to make up
2.	搭档	（名）	dādàng	partner
3.	向导	（名）	xiàngdǎo	guide
4.	俗话	（名）	súhuà	saying
5.	来劲		lái jìn	in high spirits, take something seriously
6.	朝	（介）	cháo	towards
7.	美食	（名）	měishí	delicacy
8.	简直	（副）	jiǎnzhí	simply
9.	幸福	（形）	xìngfú	happy
10.	景观	（名）	jǐngguān	landscape, scenery

注释　Notes

1. 她的妆化得真不错。

在这个句子中，"真不错"是补充说明动词"化"的程度。这种补充说明动作达到的程度的成分称为程度补语。程度补语和动词之间一般要用结构助词"得"来连接。

"真不错" is used to show the degree of the verb "化". Such a component is called complement of degree. It is connected with the verb by "得".

基本句式为：

The basic pattern is:

主语——谓语（动词／形容词）——得——程度补语

Subject—predicate (verb/adjective) —得—complement of degree

他　　　　唱　　　　得　　　不错。

否定式是在程度补语前加"不"。

The negation is formed by adding "不" in front of the complement.

例如：他说得不好。

如果动词后带有宾语，一般要重复动词。

If a verb takes both object and complement of degree, the verb has to be repeated.

例如：他说汉语说得很流利。

2. 看你能不能投中。

"中"，读第四声，这里是动词"投"的补语，表示"正对上"。

"中"，read in its fourth tone, is the complement of the verb "投", meaning "hitting the target".

例如：他打中目标了。

3. 你就别老让我读书了吧!

这是一个兼语句。在谓语部分，"我"既是动词"让"的宾语，同时又兼做动词"读书"的主语，所以称为兼语。这种句子常见的第一个动词有"请"、"叫"、"让"等。

In this sentence, "我" is both the object of "让" and the subject of "读书". Therefore, "我" is called a pivot. "请", "叫", "让" etc. are often used in this kind of sentence.

例如：今天晚上他请我吃饭。

你叫他来，我有事找他。

我让他去买东西了。

4. 这些鱼哪儿是在吃食，简直就是在抢食儿!

"哪儿"这里只表示反问语气，有否定的意思，没有处所意义。

"哪儿" here is used in a rhetorical sentence with a negative meaning.

例如：他哪儿是北京人? 他是上海人。

"简直"，副词，强调完全如此或差不多如此，含有夸张语气。

"简直", an adverb, is used for emphasis, with a bit of exaggeration.

例如：今天怎么这么热，简直像夏天。

5. 可是柳树跟听觉又有什么关系啊?

"跟"，介词，引出动作所涉及的对象。

"跟", a preposition, elicits the object of the action.

例如：这事儿跟我有什么关系?

6. "上有天堂，下有苏杭"，果然不假。

"果然"，副词，表示事实与所说或所预料的相符合。

"果然", an adverb, is used to mean "just as expected".

例如：吃了几天药，他的病果然好了。

替换练习 Substitution Drills

1. 花港	的	鱼	真是太	幸福	了。
西湖		景色		美	
北京		烤鸭		好吃	
上海		夏天		热	

2. 祝	朋友们	学习进步。
	你们	身体健康
	大家	工作顺利
	他们	新年快乐

会话 Conversations

完成下列会话 Complete the following dialogues
（如括号里有词语或提示，请按要求做 Use words or expressions given in the brackets）

A：花港那里有什么可看的。

B：＿＿＿＿＿＿＿＿＿＿＿＿＿＿＿＿＿＿。（……极了）

A：除了红鲤鱼还有别的东西可看吗？

B：＿＿＿＿＿＿＿＿＿＿＿＿＿＿＿＿＿＿。（不光……还……）

A："柳浪闻莺"是什么意思？

B：＿＿＿＿＿＿＿＿＿＿＿＿＿＿＿＿＿＿。（跟……有关系）

A：沿岸有多少棵柳树？

B：500 多棵。

杭州【第三集】

雷峰塔遗址

韩　佳：哎，大牛呢？大牛！

大　牛：哎，韩佳，韩佳，咱们这是在哪儿啊？

韩　佳：你猜我们在哪儿？

大　牛：我猜，我猜我也猜不出来①。你快告诉我吧！

韩　佳：别急嘛！我们今天《快乐中国》呢，就是要带观
　　　　众朋友们游览这个地方，所以有的是时间②。

大　牛：啊！节目已经开始啦？

韩　佳：对呀！

大　牛：大家好，这里是《快乐中国》，我是快乐的大牛。
　　　　今天我们就到……哎，到那边去看看吧。

Han Jia: Hey, where is Daniel? Daniel.

Daniel: Hey, Han Jia, Han Jia. Where are we?

Han Jia: Guess where we are.

Daniel: I don't know. Tell me, please.

Han Jia: Don't worry. In today's Happy China, we will take the audience to visit this place. So we have plenty of time.

Daniel: Wow, the program has begun.

Han Jia: Yes.

Daniel: Hello, everyone! Welcome to Happy China. I am happy Daniel. Today we are going to... Hey, let's go over there and take a look.

韩　佳：大牛，你是不是觉得今天我们看的风景有点奇怪呀③？

大　牛：有点奇怪？简直是太奇怪了！

韩　佳：告诉你吧，现在我们看的地方，是杭州有名的雷峰塔。

大　牛：啊，不会是白娘子这个故事里面的雷峰塔吧？

韩　佳：大牛，你真牛！连白娘子的故事你都知道啊④！

大　牛：那是！这叫"人不可貌相，海水不可斗量"。

Rén bùkě màoxiàng, hǎishuǐ bùkě dǒu liáng.

人 不可 貌相， 海水 不可 斗 量。

You can't judge a book by its cover.

大　牛：可是，韩佳，我听说杭州的雷峰塔可是值得一看。它怎么会
　　　　是这个样子呀⑤？不会是你弄错了吧？

韩　佳：我可没弄错！雷峰塔在历史上倒塌过几次，我们现在看到的
　　　　这个遗址，是在最后一次1924年倒塌后所留下的。

大　牛：哦，原来这里是旧的雷峰塔遗址啊！那这里还有什么值得看
　　　　的呀？

韩　佳：你呀，真是身在其中，不知道雷峰塔的壮观。走，我带你到
　　　　外边看看去！

Han Jia: Daniel, do you think the views we see today are a little weird?

Daniel: A little weird? It is too weird.

Han Jia: OK. Let me tell you. We are now at the famous Leifeng Pagoda in Hangzhou.

Daniel: Wow, is it the Leifeng Pagoda in the story of Ms. Bai?

Han Jia: Daniel, you are so smart. You even know the story of Ms. Bai.

Daniel: Of course. A man cannot be judged by his appearance, nor can the water in the sea be measured by a bucket.

Daniel: But, Han Jia, Leifeng Pagoda in Hangzhou is really worth seeing. Why is it like this? Did you make a mistake?

Han Jia: No. Leifeng Pagoda was destroyed several times throughout history. The relics we see now were left after the latest collapse in 1924.

Daniel: Oh, so it is the relics of the old Leifeng Pagoda. Then is there anything else worth seeing?

Han Jia: You are in it, but you don't know the grandeur of Leifeng Pagoda. Come on. Let's go outside to take a look.

杭州

大　牛：咦，这儿又是什么塔呀？

韩　佳：这是重建的雷峰新塔。

大　牛：雷峰新塔是怎么回事啊？

韩　佳：2002 年的时候啊，杭州重建雷峰塔了。那么它的新塔呢，
　　　　就建在了旧塔遗址的上面，而且它第一层的底下，是玻璃防
　　　　护罩。这样我们就可以身处新塔之中，饱览旧塔遗址了。

大　牛：那么，我们在这里参观就像是穿越了时空隧道一样。

Daniel: Hey, what pagoda is this?

Han Jia: It is the rebuilt new Leifeng Pagoda.

Daniel: What is the new Leifeng Pagoda?

Han Jia: In 2002, a new Leifeng Pagoda was built in Hangzhou. Where is the new pagoda? It was built on the relics of the old one. Under the ground floor, there is a glass protective shield. In this way, we can stay in the new pagoda and see the relics of the old one.

Daniel: Then when we take a tour here, We will be like taking a time machine.

场景 Scene　　新雷峰塔内

韩　佳：哎，大牛，告诉你啊，这雷峰塔上面有《白蛇传》的全景展现。

大　牛：《白蛇传》全景展现？

韩　佳：对！

大　牛：什么？要唱京剧了？

韩　佳：哟，你还看过京剧的《白蛇传》哪！

大　牛：不仅是看过，我还专门拜师学艺演过呢⑥！

韩　佳：真的？那你演谁？

大　牛：我这么才华横溢、英俊潇洒，你觉得我演谁最合适呢？

韩　佳：这么说，你演的肯定是许仙。

大　牛：我演的就是许仙……

韩　佳：哇，大牛太棒了！

大　牛：他药铺里的小伙计。

韩　佳：大牛，你这爱吹牛的毛病得改一改了吧！

Nǐ zhè ài chuī niú de máobìng děi gǎi yi gǎi le ba!
你 这 爱 吹 牛 的 毛病 得 改 一 改 了 吧!

**You really should change your awful habit of boasting,
don't you think?**

Han Jia: Hey, Daniel, let me tell you that on Leifeng Pagoda, there is a panoramic display of The Legend of the White Snake.

Daniel: The panoramic display of The Legend of the White Snake?

Han Jia: Yes.

Daniel: What? Are we going to watch Peking opera?

Han Jia: Hey, you have even watched the Peking opera of The Legend of the White Snake.

Daniel: Not only have I watched it, but also learned it from a master and played a role.

Han Jia: Really? Which part did you play?

Daniel: I am so talented and handsome. Which part do you think suits me the best?

Han Jia: Then you must have played the part of Xu Xian.

Daniel: Yes, I played the part of Xu Xian...

Han Jia: Hey, Daniel, you are so great!

Daniel: A boy working in Xu Xian's pharmacy.

Han Jia: Daniel, you'd better get rid of the habit of boasting.

新雷峰塔木雕层

大　牛：韩佳，有句话叫作"建筑是静止的音乐"。这里简直是"静止的戏剧"，太精彩了！

韩　佳：嗯，这里用静止的形式，表现了一个悲欢离合的故事。你看这一幅，这幅讲的是和雷峰塔息息相关的塔压白娘子的故事。

大　牛：哎，这个就是法海和尚吧？

韩　佳：嗯，我们今天真可以说是大饱眼福了！这六尊雕塑都是著名的东阳木雕。

大　牛：为什么叫"东阳木雕"呢？

韩　佳："东阳"是个地名，也属于浙江省。在那儿出的木雕，当然叫"东阳木雕"了。

大　牛：哎呀，雕出那么复杂的图案来，可真不容易！

韩　佳：是啊，这些木雕真可以说是精雕细刻。

Zhèxiē mùdiāo zhēn kěyǐ shuō shì jīng diāo xì kè.
这些 木雕 真 可以 说 是 精 雕 细 刻。

These wooden carvings are very delicate and refined.

Daniel: Han Jia, there is a saying "Architecture is the quiescent music". It is the quiescent opera here. So wonderful!

Han Jia: Right. It uses quiescent pattern to show a story of joys and sorrows, partings and reunions. Look at this one. It depicts the story of the pagoda suppressing Ms. Bai closely related to Leifeng Pagoda.

Daniel: Hey, this is Monk Fahai, isn't it?

Han Jia: Hey, today we really expanded our views. These six sculptures are famous Dongyang wood carvings.

Daniel: Why are they called Dongyang wood carvings?

Han Jia: Dongyang is the name of a place. It is also in Zhejiang Province. Wood carvings made there are certainly called Dongyang wood carvings.

Daniel: Hey, it is really hard to carve such complicated Patterns.

Han Jia: Right. These wood carvings are very exquisite and refined.

新雷峰塔顶层内

大　牛：哇，新雷峰塔顶层上，满眼都是金色。哎，有一个成语怎么说来着⑦? 好像是金色的墙壁还是……

韩　佳：哦，"金碧辉煌"。

大　牛：对，"金碧辉煌"。

韩　佳：哎，大牛，这雷峰塔的顶层啊，可是观赏杭州美景的绝佳地点。

大　牛："绝佳"? 跟韩佳有什么关系吗?

韩　佳：没关系。"绝"是"最"的意思，"佳"是"好"的意思。

大　牛：哦，"绝佳"就是最好。走，看风景去!

新雷峰塔顶层外

大　牛：站在雷峰塔顶上，看着杭州西湖烟雨蒙蒙的景色，真是别有一番情趣!

韩　佳：嗯，要是赶上晴天啊，每当夕阳西下的时候，你就会看到杭州很著名的一道风景——雷峰夕照。

大　牛：我可是看不够! 好，下面要进入我们今天的"赏心悦目"，好好欣赏一下吧!

韩　佳：好建议!

Daniel: Wow, the top of the new Leifeng Pagoda is all in the color of gold. Hey, there is an idiom. It is something like gold walls or...

Han Jia: Oh, "jinbi huihuang".

Daniel: Right. Splendid and magnificent.

Han Jia: Hey, Daniel, the top of Leifeng Pagoda is the perfect place to see the beautiful views of Hangzhou.

Daniel: "Juejia"? Does it have anything to do with Han Jia?

Han Jia: No. "Jue" means to the highest degree. "Jia" means good.

Daniel: Oh, "juejia" means the best. Come on. Let's go and enjoy the views.

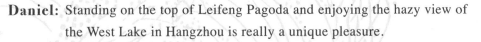

Daniel: Standing on the top of Leifeng Pagoda and enjoying the hazy view of the West Lake in Hangzhou is really a unique pleasure.

Han Jia: Right. At dusk on a sunny day, you will be able to see a very famous view of Hangzhou—Leifeng Pagoda in the Evening Glow.

Daniel: I can't have enough. OK. Next we are going to today's Feast for the Eyes to enjoy the beautiful scenery.

Han Jia: Good idea.

生词　Words and Expressions

1. 遗址	（名）	yízhǐ	ruins, relics
2. 壮观	（形）	zhuàngguān	magnificent-looking
3. 英俊	（形）	yīngjùn	handsome and smart
4. 才华	（名）	cáihuá	talent
5. 潇洒	（形）	xiāosǎ	elegand and unconventional
6. 吹牛		chuī niú	to brag about
7. 毛病	（名）	máobìng	defect
8. 精彩	（形）	jīngcǎi	excellent
9. 木雕	（名）	mùdiāo	wood sculpture
10. 精雕细刻		jīng diāo xì kè	carve with care and precision

注释　Notes

1. 我猜我也猜不出来。

这里的"出来"表示事物随动作由隐蔽到显露。

"出来" is used to express that things or events appear from obscurity.

例如：我认出来了，他是我小学的同学。

2. 所以有的是时间。

"有的是"是习惯用语，表示数量很多。

"有的是"，a colloquial expression，means a large quantity.

例如：这种词典，书店里有的是。

3. 你是不是觉得今天我们看的风景有点儿奇怪呀？

"有点儿"，副词，表示程度不高，多用于不如意的事情。

"有点儿"，an adverb，means "a little bit"，"slightly"，it is usually used to modify something unsatisfactory.

例如：他没有准备好，所以今天考试的时候，他有点儿紧张。

4. 连白娘子的故事你都知道呀！

"连……都（也）……"这一结构常用来表示强调，所要强调的成分放在"连……都（也）"中间。

The structure "连……都（也）……" is often used for emphasis，and what is being emphasized is put in between "连……都（也）".

例如：他学了一年汉语了，可是连这几句简单的话他都听不懂。

5. 它怎么会是这个样子呀？

这是一个反问句，"怎么"这里只表示反问语气，不表示方式。全句的意思是"它不会是这个样子。"

"怎么" is used in a rhetorical sentence，having lost its original function as asking about the manner. The meaning of the whole sentence is "it can't be like this".

例如：你怎么能这样说话呢？

6. 不仅是看过，我还专门拜师学艺演过呢！

这是一个递进复句，"不仅……还……"连接两个分句，后一分句比前一分句表达更进一层的意思。

The structure "不仅……还……"，similar to "not only... but also..."，is a progressive compound sentence. The latter clause further expresses the meaning of the former one.

例如：他不仅喜欢杭州，还打算在杭州生活一段时间。

7. 有一个成语怎么说来着？

"来着"，助词，表示曾经发生过什么事情，用于口语。

"来着"，an auxiliary word，is used in spoken Chinese to mean something has happened.

例如：去年春节咱们干什么来着？

替换练习　Substitution Drills

1. 你这爱　　吹牛　　　　的毛病得改一改了吧!
　　　　　　偷懒
　　　　　　虚荣
　　　　　　花钱

- -

2. 这些　　木雕　　　真可以说是　　精雕细刻。
　　　　　书法　　　　　　　　　　一流的作品
　　　　　建筑　　　　　　　　　　建筑史上的杰作
　　　　　展品　　　　　　　　　　琳琅满目

会话　Conversations

完成下列会话 Complete the following dialogues
(如括号里有词语或提示，请按要求做 Use words or expressions given in the brackets)

A: 你看过京剧《白蛇传》吗?
B: 我 _____。(不仅……还……)
B: 那你演谁呀?
A: 我演 _____。

- -

A: 你游览过西湖吗?
B: 我游览过好几次了。
A: 那你对西湖的景点很熟悉了。
B: 没错, _____。(连……也……)

杭州

万松书院牌坊

韩 佳：哎，大牛，今天啊，我带你去一所名校看看。

大 牛：哦，一个有名的学校？我可是中国人民大学的优秀毕业生，
我最爱学习了。那这个学校在哪儿啊？

韩 佳：就在山上啊，特别有名。走！

大 牛：哦，在山上的学校，环境一定很优美！

Han Jia: Hey, Daniel, today, I will take you to visit a famous school.

Daniel: Oh? A famous school? I am an excellent graduate from Renmin University of China. I love study the most. Where is the school?

Han Jia: It's on the hill. It's very famous. Come on.

Daniel: Oh? A school on the hill? The surroundings must be very beautiful.

"品"字牌坊

韩　佳：大牛，我们到了！

大　牛：哎，韩佳，搞错了吧？那里写着"书院"两个字，这里一定不是什么学校，是图书馆吧？这个图书馆还不小。

韩　佳：大牛，"书院"就是学校，只不过是古时候的学校。这所万松书院啊，早在明朝的时候就已经有了。

大　牛：哦，我知道了，古代人们把学校叫"书院"。"书"是一声，"院"是四声，"书院"。不过，韩佳，这还是我第一次看到一所名校的前面立着三块牌坊。

韩　佳：这三块牌坊啊，可是万松书院的标志性建筑。你看，它们一排列，就成了一个"品"字。一，二，三。

大　牛："品"，三个口。哦，我知道了，中国古代做官，是按照"品"来分级别的。比如说有"一品大人"、"七品官"。品数越小，官越大①。

韩　佳：嗯，说得没错！不过呢，你刚才说的这个"品"是等级的意思。但是这里的三块牌坊排成的"品"，是品德、品质的意思，也就包含着"做人要有人品，做官要有官品"的寓意。

Zuò rén yào yǒu rénpǐn, zuò guān yào yǒu guānpǐn.
做 人 要 有 人 品， 做 官 要 有 官 品。

People should be of good character, officials should have high moral standards.

Han Jia: Daniel, here we are.

Daniel: Hey, Han Jia, did you make a mistake? It is inscribed with two characters "Shu Yuan". It can't be a school. It must be a library. It is a big library.

Han Jia: Daniel, "shuyuan" means school, a school in ancient times. This Wansong Academy of Classical Learning was built in the Ming Dynasty.

Daniel: Oh, I see. In ancient China, people called schools "shuyuan", "shu" with a first tone, "yuan" with a fourth tone. But, Han Jia, I have never seen three memorial archways in front of a famous school.

Han Jia: These archways are the symbolic structure of Wansong Academy of Classical Learning. Look, they are arranged in a way to form the character "Pin". One, two, three.

Daniel: "Pin", three mouths. Well, I see. Ancient Chinese officials were ranked by "pin". For example, "yipin daren", "qipin guan". The smaller the number was the higher the rank was.

Han Jia: Right. The "pin" you mentioned means grade. But the "pin" formed by the three archways means moral character or trait. It indicates people should be of good character, and officials should have high moral standards.

室内立体微缩雕塑

大　牛：哎，韩佳，这些小人儿、小房子真好玩儿啊！

韩　佳：你可不要光看热闹啊②，这些都是我们学习的榜样。

大　牛：哦，什么是"榜样"啊？

韩　佳："榜样"就是值得学习的人或事。

大　牛：我知道，"榜"是三声，"样"是四声，意思是模范、典型。
　　　　那韩佳，这里有哪些榜样呢？

韩　佳：你看这个，这讲的是"凿壁借光"的故事。中国汉代有个叫
　　　　匡衡的人，他家里特别穷，点不起灯③。为了读书呢，他只
　　　　能请求邻居在墙壁上能凿一个洞，这样的话，他就能借邻居
　　　　家的灯光来读书了。

大　牛：哇，这么刻苦啊！

Daniel: Hey, Han Jia. These tiny figures and houses are so interesting.

Han Jia: Don't just look at them for fun. They are our "bangyang" and we should learn from them.

Daniel: Well, what is "bangyang"?

Han Jia: "Bangyang" means people or things worth learning from.

Daniel: Oh, I see. "Bangyang", third tone, fourth tone, means a paragon or a model. Han Jia, what paragons are they?

Han Jia: Look at this one. It tells the story of "zao bi jie guang". In the Han Dynasty, there was a man named Kuang Heng. He was very poor and could not afford a lamp. In order to read, he had to ask his neighbor to knock a hole on the wall. In this way, he was able to read books by the light from his neighbor's house.

Daniel: Wow, he studied so hard.

梁山伯、祝英台读书院

大　牛：哎，韩佳，这万松书院成才的人还真不少啊！

韩　佳：是不少！哎，其中有两位你肯定知道。

大　牛：哪两位？

韩　佳：梁山伯和祝英台啊！

大　牛：哎呀，这两位我怎能不知道，这可是个美丽的故事！祝英台女扮男装和梁山伯一起读书，后来两个人就相爱了。

韩　佳：嗯，他们俩就是在这万松书院一块儿读书的，只可惜是个悲剧，到最后他们俩也没能成婚。死后化作美丽的蝴蝶比翼双飞。

大　牛：哎，韩佳，前几天刚听到了许仙和白娘子的故事，今天我们就来到了梁山伯和祝英台读书的书院，杭州可真是个浪漫的城市！

Hángzhōu kě zhēn shì yí ge làngmàn de chéngshì！

杭州　可真是一个　浪漫　的　城市！

Hangzhou really is a romantic city.

大　牛：不过，他们俩做同学做三年了，梁山伯怎么可能看不出来是男是女啊？

韩　佳：能不能看出来，一会儿去了他们的书房你就知道了。

Daniel: Hey, Han Jia. Wansong Academy of Classical Learning had cultivated so many talented people.

Han Jia: Yes. Hey, I'm sure you know two of them.

Daniel: Which two?

Han Jia: Liang Shanbo and Zhu Yingtai.

Daniel: Well, I certainly know them. It is a touching story. Zhu Yingtai disguised herself as a boy and went to school with Liang Shanbo. Later, the two fell in love with each other.

Han Jia: well, they went to school together at Wansong Academy of Classical Learning. Unfortunately, it was a tragedy and they could not get married. After they died, they transformed into beautiful butterflies and flied together.

Daniel: Hey, Han Jia. A couple of days ago, I heard the story about Xu Xian and Ms. Bai. Today, we came to the school that Liang Shanbo and Zhu Yingtai once studied in. Hangzhou is really a romantic city.

Daniel: But, they had been schoolmates for three years. How come Liang Shanbo didn't find out that Zhu Yingtai was a girl?

Han Jia: Once you go to their study, you will find it out.

梁祝书房

韩　佳：大牛，你看，这就是梁山伯和祝英台了。

大　牛：好，我来看看谁是祝英台、谁是梁山伯。这个梁山伯，太不注意观察了！祝英台明明是女的，我一眼就看出来了④。

Wǒ yì yǎn jiù kàn chulai le.
我 一 眼 就 看 出来 了。

I knew as soon as I saw.

韩　佳：那你从哪儿看出来的啊？

大　牛：你看，她的眉毛，她的眼睛，有一个词儿……

韩　佳："眉清目秀"，是吧？

大　牛：对，"眉清目秀"。"眉"就是眉毛，"目"就是眼睛，"眉清目秀"就是形容人长得清秀。当然了，韩佳，你也是眉清目秀。

韩　佳：其实，大牛啊看得也不够仔细。您瞧，真正的秘密在这儿呢！古时候的女孩子都要戴耳环，所以呢，祝英台的耳垂上面也扎了个眼儿。

Han Jia: Daniel, look, these are Liang Shanbo and Zhu Yingtai.

Daniel: All right. Let me see who is Zhu Yingtai and who is Liang Shanbo. Liang Shanbo didn't make careful observation. Zhu Yingtai was obviously a girl. I found it out at the first sight.

Han Jia: How did you find it out?

Daniel: Look, her brows, her eyes. There is a phrase...

Han Jia: "Mei qing mu xiu", isn't it?

Daniel: Right. Delicate brows and pretty eyes. "Mei" means eyebrows, "mu" means eyes, "mei qing mu xiu" describes someone who has a beautiful face. Of course, Han Jia, you also have delicate brows and pretty eyes.

Han Jia: Actually, Daniel, you didn't make a careful observation either. Look, the true secret lies here. In ancient times, all girls wore earrings. So Zhu Yingtai's earlobes were pierced too.

读书台

韩 佳：哎，大牛，这里就是万松书院的读书台了。

大 牛：古代人真是太有福气了！你看这里既安静又能看到西湖的
　　　美景⑤，真是难得的好地方！

韩 佳：嗯，既然这里是个读书的好地方，那我看，你就留在这里发
　　　奋读书，争取早日成才⑥！

大 牛：别，别，别！人家都说："人行千里路，胜读十年书。"我还
　　　是接着跟你游杭州吧。

韩 佳：你还真会找理由！那好吧，明天我们继续游杭州。

Han Jia: Hey, Daniel, this is the study platform of Wansong.

Daniel: Ancient people were lucky. It is quiet here and you can also enjoy the beautiful views of the West Lake. It is really a good place.

Han Jia: Right. It is a good place to study. I think you'd better stay here to study hard, and try to become a talent as soon as possible.

Daniel: No, no, no. People say that a one-thousand-li trip is far more useful than ten years of study. Let me continue the tour in Hangzhou with you.

Han Jia: You found a perfect excuse. All right. Let's continue our tour in Hangzhou tomorrow.

生词　Words and Expressions

1. 书院　　（名）　　shūyuàn　　academy for classical studies
2. 人品　　（名）　　rénpǐn　　moral standing
3. 寓意　　（名）　　yùyì　　implied meaning, moral
4. 榜样　　（名）　　bǎngyàng　　model
5. 刻苦　　（形）　　kèkǔ　　hardworking
6. 成才　　（动）　　chéngcái　　to become a useful person
7. 悲剧　　（名）　　bēijù　　tragedy
8. 比翼双飞　　　　bǐ yì shuāng fēi　　fly wing by wing
9. 浪漫　　（形）　　làngmàn　　romantic
10. 耳环　　（名）　　ěrhuán　　earring

注释　Notes

1. 品数越小，官越大。

"越……越……"表示后者随着前者的变化而变化。

"越……越……" is similar to "the more... the more...", the thing after the second "越" changes as the thing after the first "越" changes.

例如：问题越争论越清楚。

2. 你可不要光看热闹啊……

"光"，副词，"只"的意思。

"光", an adverb, means "only".

例如：这个孩子一天到晚光想着玩儿，不想学习。

3. 他家里特别穷，点不起灯。

"起"是动词"点"的补语，否定形式为"不起"，表示不能承受；肯定形式为"点得起"。

"起" is a complement to the verb "点" and its negative form is "不起", meaning "cannot afford". Its affirmative form is "点得起".

例如：我买不起这么贵的衣服。

4. 祝英台明明是女的，我一眼就看出来了。

　　"明明"，副词，表示显然是这样。

　　"明明"，an adverb，means "obviously"。

　　例如：你明明知道九点钟开会，你为什么这时候才来？

　　"一眼"，意思是用眼睛看一下，表示时间非常短。

　　"一眼"，means "at a single glance"。

　　例如：你从门口走过去的时候，我一眼就看出来是你了。

5. 这里既安静又能看到西湖的美景……

　　"既……又……"，表示两种情况都有。

　　"既……又……"，similar to "both... and..."，indicates both situations exist。

　　例如：这个学生既聪明又勤奋，学习成绩一直很好。

6. 既然这里是个读书的好地方，那我看你就留在这里发奋读书，争取早日成才！

　　"既然"，连词，多用在上句的开头，下句里常用"就"、"也"、"还"跟它相呼应，上句提出前提，下句加以推论。

　　"既然"，a conjunction，meaning "now that" or "since"。It is often used in the beginning of the first clause，and "就，也，还" are often used in the second clause. The first clause provides the premise，while the second gives the inference.

　　例如：你既然不喜欢就不要买了。

替换练习 Substitution Drills

1. 我一眼就看　　出来　　了。
　　　　　　　　到
　　　　　　　　穿
　　　　　　　　清楚

* *

2. 杭州　　　　可真是一个　　浪漫　　　　的　　　城市。
　　北京大学　　　　　　　　历史悠久　　　　　　学校
　　王家村　　　　　　　　　富裕　　　　　　　　村庄
　　工人体育场　　　　　　　现代化　　　　　　　体育场所

会话　Conversations

完成下列会话 Complete the following dialogues
（如括号里有词语或提示，请按要求做 Use words or expressions given in the brackets）

A：这次游览西湖，你觉得怎么样？

B：太有意思了，_____。（既……又……）

A：是啊。美丽的景色和浪漫的传说故事是西湖的两大特点。

B：以后有机会我还要来。

杭州

【第五集】

河坊街

大　牛：今天韩佳带我来到了杭州的一条古街，这条古街的名字就叫
　　　　做……

韩　佳：河坊街。

大　牛：对，河坊街。哇，这河坊街真是名不虚传啊！两边的店铺都
　　　　看上去很古老啊①！

韩　佳：是啊，这河坊街两边的店铺，可都是老字号。

大　牛：哎，真精致啊！这叫什么？

韩　佳：面人儿啊！你瞧，师傅正在捏面人儿②。

大　牛：哦，捏面人儿。

韩　佳：对，捏面人是中国民间的一门手艺。

Niē miànrén shì Zhōngguó mínjiān de yì mén shǒuyì.
捏　面人　是　中国　　民间　的　一　门　手艺。

Sculpting dough figurines is a traditional Chinese folk art.

66

Daniel: Today, Han Jia took me to an old street in Hangzhou. The name of the old street is...

Han Jia: Hefang Street.

Daniel: Right. Hefang Street. Wow, Hefang Street is true to its fame. The stores on both sides look so old.

Han Jia: Yes. The stores on both sides of Hefang Street are old brand stores.

Daniel: Wow, so exquisite. What is it called?

Han Jia: Dough figurine. Look, the master is making a dough figurine.

Daniel: Oh, dough figurine.

Han Jia: Right. Dough figurine is a folk handcraft in China.

许仙药铺门口

大　牛：虽然不是特别像我，但是我还是很喜欢。

韩　佳：别陶醉啦！抬头看看，你可是故地重游啊！

大　牛：可是，韩佳，我从来没来过这里呀！

韩　佳：哎，这个铜人你应该认识吧？

大　牛：他是谁呀？

韩　佳：许仙啊！

大　牛：他就是许仙啊！

韩　佳：对呀！

大　牛：哎，韩佳，我以前扮演过许仙……药铺里的小伙计呢。

韩　佳：这个大牛。哎，这里就是许仙药铺了，走，上你们店里瞧瞧去！

大　牛：好，好，好！

许仙药铺店堂内

大　牛：来，韩佳，请！哎，大家好，大家好！我走了之后，生意还是不错吧？她们都太忙了，顾不上咱们了③。哎，韩佳，你今天来了，一定要多买点药材啊！照顾照顾我们的生意。给这位顾客打八折！

韩　佳：谢了，谢了！我今天不想买药。

大　牛：那好吧，咱们到别的地方逛逛去。

Daniel: It does not look like me very much, but I love it anyway.

Han Jia: Stop intoxicating yourself. Look up. You are visiting this place once again.

Daniel: But, Han Jia, I have never been here before.

Han Jia: Hey, do you recognize the bronze figure?

Daniel: Who is he?

Han Jia: Xu Xian.

Daniel: He is Xu Xian?

Han Jia: Right.

Daniel: Hey, Han Jia, I once played a role as a boy working in Xu Xian's pharmacy.

Han Jia: Daniel. Hey, here is Xu Xian's pharmacy. Let's go inside and take a look.

Daniel: OK.

Daniel: Come on. Han Jia. Please. Hey, hello. Has the business been ok since I left? They are too busy to take care of us. Hey, Han Jia, since you are here today, you should buy a lot of herbal medicines in favor of our business. Give this customer a 20% discount.

Han Jia: Thank you, but I don't want to buy medicine today.

Daniel: All right. Let's go to see some other places.

河坊街

韩　佳：哎，这条街上面还有另外一间和它同样有名的药铺，你看！

大　牛：啊，好大的字！"胡庆余堂"。

韩　佳：嗯，没错，这是清朝末期有名的商人胡雪岩的药铺。你看这招牌，够气派的吧！

Nǐ kàn zhè kuài zhāopai, gòu qìpài de ba!
你 看 这 块 招牌， 够 气派 的 吧！

Look at this shop sign, pretty impressive, wouldn't you say?

韩　佳：哎，它可是你们许氏药店的有力竞争者呀！

大　牛：不怕，不怕！各有特色嘛，而且有竞争才能有进步嘛！

韩　佳：想不到这大牛还真有商业头脑。

大　牛：那当然，我自己还想着到河坊街来开一家店铺什么的④。那样的话，我每天都能看到西湖的美景了。

韩　佳：嗯，这个主意不错，哎，你看，那儿的伞多漂亮啊！

大　牛：哎，有了。我开一个卖伞的店铺也不错。看看去！

Han Jia: There is another pharmacy of the same fame as this one. Look.

Daniel: Wow, what big characters—Hu Qing Yu Tang.

Han Jia: Right. It is the pharmacy of the famous merchant Hu Xueyan born at the end of the Qing Dynasty. Look at this shop sign. Pretty impressive, wouldn't you say?

Han Jia: Hey, it is a competitive rival of Xu's pharmacy.

Daniel: Don't worry. We have different features. Besides, only in competition can we make progress.

Han Jia: I didn't expect Daniel would have such a good business insight.

Daniel: Of course. I myself would like to open a store on Hefang Street, so I can enjoy the beautiful views of the West Lake everyday.

Han Jia: Right. Good idea. Hey, look, the umbrellas are so nice.

Daniel: Hey, I've got an idea. It would be nice to open an umbrella store. Go over and take a look.

场景 Scene　伞铺

韩　佳：哎，大牛，你看这些伞好看吗？

大　牛：太好看了！

大　牛：哎，老板，这里的伞卖得怎么样啊？

韩　佳：那还用问⑤，这西湖绸伞啊，可是中国伞中的精品，当然卖得好了。

卖伞人：是啊，人们一般把西湖绸伞比做西湖之花呢！

大　牛：哦，样式还真不少！这些都有什么用处呢？

卖伞人：这个是装饰的，这个是挡太阳的，这个是挡雨的。

大　牛：这个是装饰的。

韩　佳：这是挡太阳的。

大　牛：嗯，挡太阳的英文里叫 parasol，那么挡雨的叫 umbrella。

韩　佳：没想到这个大牛还挺好学的，居然在这里学起做伞来了。看来我也应该学一门手艺。哎，有了，前面有一家有名的老字号——王星记扇子店，我去那儿看看。

大　牛：哎，韩佳，韩佳，等等我，我也要去！

韩　佳：那你不学做伞了？

大　牛：学呀，但是我还想看看扇子，学得多，会的多嘛。

韩　佳：中国有句俗语说得好：艺不压身。说的就是多学点没坏处。

yì　bù　yā　shēn
艺　不　压　身

It doesn't hurt to learn more.

Han Jia: Hey, Daniel, do you think these umbrellas are nice?

Daniel: They are great!

Daniel: Hey, Madame, how is the business?

Han Jia: Needless to say, the silk umbrella of the West Lake is the masterpiece of Chinese umbrellas. Of course the business is good.

Saleswoman: Right. People usually call the silk umbrellas as the West Lake flowers.

Daniel: Well, there are so many varieties. What are they used for?

Saleswoman: This is for decoration. This is for sun shielding. This is for rain shielding.

Daniel: This is for decoration.

Han Jia: This is for sun shielding.

Daniel: Right. Sun-shielding umbrellas in English are called parasol. Rain-shielding umbrellas in English are called umbrella.

Han Jia: I didn't expect that Daniel is so fond of learning. He even learned to make umbrellas here. It seems that I should learn a handcraft too. Hey, I've got an idea. There is a famous old brand store ahead. Wang Xingji Fan Store. I will go there and check it out.

Daniel: Hey, Han Jia, wait for me. I am going with you.

Han Jia: Won't you learn to make umbrellas?

Daniel: Yes. But I would like to see the fans too. If I learn more, I will know more.

Han Jia: There is an old Chinese saying, "yi bu ya shen". It means it doesn't hurt to learn more.

王星记扇子店

大　牛：哇，这么多扇子！

韩　佳：三伏天里手拿折扇，真是又惬意又潇洒！

大　牛：嗯，我们说伞或者扇子的时候，都可以用"把"这个量词。哎，那是什么香味？

韩　佳：当然是我手中的这把檀香扇了！这种扇子即使用上十年，也依然有扑鼻的香味⑥。

大　牛：哇，真是很神奇啊！

韩　佳：哎，你再来看看这把，怎么样？

大　牛：黑色，不好看！

韩　佳：哎，你可不要小瞧它，这是有名的黑纸扇。这种扇子不论是太阳晒，还是热水煮，都不会变形⑦。

大　牛：啊，那么结实。那我一定要买上几把送给朋友！

韩　佳：哎，别着急！我们现在呢，先带观众朋友们去看看"赏心悦目"的风景，一会儿你再慢慢挑。

Daniel: Wow, so many fans!

Han Jia: In mid summer, holding a folded fan in hand is really pleasant and elegant.

Daniel: Right. When we talk about umbrellas and fans, we can use the quantifier "ba". Hey, what is that fragrance?

Han Jia: It is from the sandalwood fan in my hand. This kind of fan will still keep the strong fragrance even after ten years of use.

Daniel: Wow, that's really marvelous!

Han Jia: Hey, come over and take a look at this one.

Daniel: Black is not a good color.

Han Jia: Hey, don't underestimate it. It's the famous black paper fan. This kind of fan won't disfigure neither in sun nor in hot water.

Daniel: Wow, so enduring. I will certainly buy some for my friends as gifts.

Han Jia: Hey, wait. Let's take the audience to see the beautiful scenery in the Feast for the Eyes first. You can pick some fans later.

生词 Words and Expressions

1. 名不虚传		míng bù xū chuán	live up to one's reputation
2. 老字号	（名）	lǎozìhao	time-honoured brand
3. 民间	（名）	mínjiān	folk
4. 手艺	（名）	shǒuyì	craftsmanship
5. 扮演	（动）	bànyǎn	to act, play the part of
6. 招牌	（名）	zhāopai	sign, tablet
7. 气派	（形）	qìpài	imposing manner
8. 伞	（名）	sǎn	umbrella
9. 扇子	（名）	shànzi	fan
10. 惬意	（形）	qièyì	to be pleased

注释 Notes

1. 两边的店铺都看上去很古老啊！

"上去"是动词"看"的补语；"看上去"表示从外表估计、打量。

"上去" serves as the complement to the verb "看"。"看上去" means to estimate from the appearance.

例如：这个人很年轻，看上去只有三十多岁。

2. 师傅正在捏面人儿。

副词"正在"或"在"用在动词或动词结构前，表示一个动作正在进行。

Adverbs "正在" and "在" are used before a verb or a verb structure to show that an action is going on. Its basic pattern is:

基本句式为：

主语——正在 / 正——谓语动词——宾语

Subject—正在 / 正—Predicate verb—Object

他们　　正在　　　　看　　　电视。

否定式用"没（有）在……"或只用"没有"。

Its negative form is "没（有）在……" or "没有".

例如：他没（在）看报纸，他在听音乐。

3. 她们太忙了，顾不上咱们了。

"顾"，动词，常带补语"得上（不上）"，意思是"照管到（不到）"、"来得及（不及）"。

"顾"，a verb, often takes its complement "上（不上）", meaning "take care of (not able to take care of)" or "there's still time for... (there is no time for...)".

例如：只剩五分钟了，小明顾不上吃饭了。

4. 我自己还想着到河坊街来开一家店铺什么的。

"什么的"用在一个成分或几个并列成分之后，相当于"等等"。

"什么的"，used after a component or several coordinate components, is similar to "and so on", "etc.".

例如：我要去商店买纸呀、笔呀什么的。

5. 那还用问……

这是一个反问句，"还"表示反问语气，有"不应该"、"没有必要"的意思。

"还" is used in a rhetorical question, meaning "there's no need to...".

例如：这样好的工作，你还不满意呀？

6. 这种扇子即使用上十年也依然有扑鼻的香味。

这是一个让步复句，"即使……也……"连接前后两部分，前一部分假设一种极端情况，后一部分表示结果不受影响。

The structure "即使……也……" is a concessional complex sentence. It is similar to "even if..." in English.

例如：这辆自行车即使骑上十年也不会坏。

7. 这种扇子不论是太阳晒，还是热水煮，都不会变形。

这是一个条件复句。"不论"为连词，后面常有"都、也、总"相呼应，说明在任何条件下结果都不会改变。

It is a conditional complex sentence. "不论……都……" is similar to "no matter how...". "不论" is a conjunction, often echoed by "都、也、总" in the latter part of the sentence.

例如：这次活动不论他参加不参加，我们的计划都不会改变。

替换练习　Substitution Drills

1. 捏面人	是中国民间的	一门手艺。
贴对联		一种风俗
踩高跷		一种娱乐活动
剪纸		一种手工艺品

2. 你看这	块	招牌，够	气派	的吧！
	座	大楼	高	
	件	衣服	漂亮	
	辆	汽车	高级	

会话　Conversations

完成下列会话 Complete the following dialogues
（如括号里有词语或提示，请按要求做 Use words or expressions given in the brackets）

A：你看杭州的商店怎么样？

B：＿＿＿＿＿＿＿＿＿＿＿＿＿＿。（看上去）

A：你看，那座大楼真高啊！

B：＿＿＿＿＿＿＿＿＿＿＿＿＿＿。（气派）

A：他很注意锻炼身体吧？

B：没错，＿＿＿＿＿＿＿＿＿＿＿。（无论……还是……都……）

A：你也每天都锻炼吗？

B：＿＿＿＿＿＿＿＿＿＿＿＿＿＿。

杭州 【第六集】

杭州街上

韩 佳：哎，大牛，你看！

大 牛：哎，韩佳，你已经请我坐船了，不用请我吃饭了。

韩 佳：你就想着吃！这是刚出的新版人民币。

大 牛：哦，我看看，才一块钱！还不够买一根冰棍儿呢！

韩 佳：哎，我是要让你看它背面的风景。

大 牛：哦，有什么风景？

韩 佳：这就是著名的"三潭印月"。

大 牛：这个景点都被印在纸币上了①，一定非常有名。

韩 佳：那当然，我们一会儿就能看见了。

Han Jia: Hey, Daniel, look.

Daniel: Hey, Han Jia, you've invited me to a cruise. You don't need to invite me to a meal any more.

Han Jia: Food is the only thing on your mind. This is the newly issued Renminbi.

Daniel: Well, let me take a look. It is a one *yuan* note. It is not even enough to buy a popsicle.

Han Jia: Hey, I want you to look at the landscape on the back.

Daniel: Well, What landscape?

Han Jia: This is the famous "Three Pools Mirroring the Moon".

Daniel: It is printed on the bill. It must be very famous.

Han Jia: Of course, we will see it in a moment.

大　牛：哎，韩佳，我想起来了②。你跟我说过，西湖上有三座岛，
　　　　其中最大的一个就是"三潭印月"吧！

韩　佳：嗯，记性还真不错。这"三潭印月"又叫"小瀛洲"。

大　牛：啊，这个"瀛"字可够难写的呀③！

韩　佳：对呀，你可数好了，这个字一共有 19 画，可别少一笔哦！

大　牛：嗯，那"小瀛洲"它有什么含义呢？

韩　佳：小瀛洲是中国古代神话中的仙山，它是人们想象中神奇、美
　　　　丽的理想世界。

Tā shì rénmen xiǎngxiàng zhōng shénqí、 měilì de lǐxiǎng shìjiè.
它 是 人们 　想象 　中 　神奇、美丽 的 理想 世界。

It's an imaginary world, beautiful, mystical and ideal.

Daniel: Hey, Han Jia, I remember something. You once told me that there are three islets on the West Lake. The biggest one is the Three Pools Mirroring the Moon.

Han Jia: Right. You have a good memory. The Three Pools Mirroring the Moon is also called Xiao Yingzhou.

Daniel: Wow, the character "Ying" is so difficult to write.

Han Jia: Yes. Count the strokes. This character has 19 strokes.

Daniel: Well, what does Xiao Yingzhou mean?

Han Jia: Xiao Yingzhou is a magic mountain in an ancient Chinese fairy tale. It is the magic, beautiful and ideal world in people's imagination.

九曲桥

韩　佳：从这座桥上面，每走一步，都能看到不一样的风景。

大　牛：嗯，这个咱们学过，叫"移步换景"。哎，韩佳，我想起来了，我们在其他地方看过很多各种各样不同造型的亭子，我发现西湖的亭子也不少。

韩　佳：西湖上面的亭子不仅造型奇特，而且它们的名字也很有意思。你看，身后这一座叫"开网亭"。

大　牛：哦，我知道了，是个钓鱼的好地方。撒大网，钓大鱼。

韩　佳：你是撒网捕鱼，人家可是在这里撒网放鱼。

大　牛：得，又露怯了！

韩　佳：这里是一个放生的地方，把鱼从这里放回湖中。哎，你听说过"网开一面"这个成语吗？

大　牛："网开一面"，听过，但是它的实际含义我不太明白。

韩　佳："网开一面"，就是说把捕捉禽兽的网打开一面，比喻用宽大的态度去对待别人。比如说，你犯的错误非常严重，但是我网开一面，就不惩罚你了。

大　牛：但是，我今天又没犯错。"网开一面"字面意思是把网打开一面，比喻放开一条生路。

wǎng　kāi　yí　miàn
网　开　一　面

to let someone off the hook

Han Jia: On this bridge, you will see a different view every time you take a new step.

Daniel: Right. We learned this before. It is called "yi bu huan jing". Hey, Han Jia, I remember. We saw a lot of pavilions in different shapes in other places. I found that there are many pavilions at the West Lake as well.

Han Jia: The pavilions at the West Lake are not only of unique designs, but also have interesting names. Look at the Kai Wang Pavilion behind you.

Daniel: Well, I know it is a perfect place for fishing. Cast large net for big fish.

Han Jia: You cast net to catch fish. But people here cast net to let the fish go.

Daniel: Oh, I was wrong again.

Han Jia: It is a place to set free the captured fish. Let the fish return to the lake. Hey, have you ever heard about the idiom "wang kai yi mian"?

Daniel: Yes, I have. But I don't really know its meaning.

Han Jia: "Wang kai yi mian" literally means leaving an opening on the net used for capturing animals. It implies treating people with a magnanimous attitude. For instance, you made a serious mistake, but I gave you a way out and would not punish you.

Daniel: But, I haven't made any mistakes today. "Wang kai yi mian" literally to open one side of the net, implying letting somebody off the hook.

亭亭亭

韩　佳：哎，亭亭亭。

大　牛：怎么了？

韩　佳：没怎么！

大　牛：走得好好的，你干吗让我停下来呀？

韩　佳：你一定是误会了，这座亭子就叫"亭亭亭"。

大　牛："亭亭亭"这是什么名字啊！

韩　佳：走到这里的确应该停下来，看看这座亭亭玉立的亭子。

大　牛：这么多个"亭"字，这个名字起得真有意思④。那好吧，咱
　　　　们就停下来，好好看看吧！

Han Jia: Hey, Tingting Pavilion.

Daniel: What's the matter?

Han Jia: Nothing.

Daniel: Why did you ask me to stop?

Han Jia: You misunderstood me. This pavilion is called Tingting Pavilion.

Daniel: Tingting Pavilion. Well, what a name it is!

Han Jia: We really need to stop here and take a look at the gorgeous pavilion.

Daniel: So many duplicates of the character "ting". It is an interesting name.
All right. Let's stop and take a good look at it.

亭 内

大　牛：这座亭子的形状有点奇怪。你看，那边是墙，另一边是走廊。

韩　佳：哎，在西湖的景区里，恐怕再也找不着第二个这样的亭子了。

大　牛：我看它根本不是亭子。

韩　佳：哎，大牛，你看那边，那里就是"三潭印月"的三座石塔了。

大　牛：哦，一，二，三。没想到这三座石塔之间的距离这么远！

韩　佳：嗯，这三座石塔构成了一个等边三角形。塔与塔之间的距离呢，是62米。

大　牛：嗯，可惜在岸上看塔看得不清楚啊。哎，韩佳，咱们是不是……

韩　佳：我就知道你又想坐船了。早就准备好了，走吧！

大　牛：游西湖哪能不坐船呢⑤？她安排得可真周到。

Tā ānpái de kě zhēn zhōudào.
她 安排 得 可 真 周到。

She's arranged everything right down to the smallest detail.

Daniel: The shape of the pavilion is odd. Look, the wall is over there, and the corridor is on the other side.

Han Jia: Hey, in the West Lake scenic area, you won't be able to find another pavilion like this.

Daniel: I don't think it is a pavilion at all.

Han Jia: Hey, Daniel, look over there. They are the three stone pagodas of the Three Pools Mirroring the Moon.

Daniel: Well, one, two, three. I didn't expect that the distance between these three pagodas is so long.

Han Jia: Right. The three pagodas form an equilateral triangle. The distance between the pagodas is 62 meters.

Daniel: Well, unfortunately, we are on the bank and cannot see the pagodas clearly. Hey, Han Jia, could we...?

Han Jia: I know you want to take a boat again. I have already made the arrangement. Let's go.

Daniel: How can we tour on the West Lake without taking a boat? She really made a nice arrangement.

韩 佳：怎么样？大牛，这回看清楚了吧！

大 牛：嗯，圆圆的塔身，上面还顶了个小葫芦。哎，韩佳，为什么要在湖的中间立三座塔呢？是因为好看吗？

韩 佳：立这三座塔，可不光是为了好看。苏东坡在湖中间最深的地方建了三座塔作为标志，规定在三座塔之内不许种莲藕。

大 牛：这是为什么呢？

韩 佳：防止西湖淤塞啊！不过咱们看到的这三座塔，是清朝的时候重建的。

大 牛：嗯，小瀛洲有湖、有塔、有桥、有亭，的确像仙境一样！

Han Jia: How is it? Daniel, can you see them clearly now?

Daniel: Yes. The round pagoda has a small gourd on the top. Hey, Han Jia, why were the three pagodas built in the middle of the lake? Is it just for the aesthetical effect?

Han Jia: No, it is not just for the aesthetical effect. Su Dongpo built three pagodas in the deepest parts of the lake as marks. He ordered that no lotus be planted between the three pagodas.

Daniel: Why?

Han Jia: It was to prevent the West Lake from being silted up. But the three pagodas we see now were rebuilt in the Qing Dynasty.

Daniel: Well, there are lakes, pagodas, bridges and pavilions at Xiao Yingzhou. It is really like a wonderland.

生词　Words and Expressions

1. 想象　（动）　xiǎngxiàng　to imagine
2. 神奇　（形）　shénqí　magical
3. 理想　（名、形）　lǐxiǎng　ideal
4. 各种各样　gè zhǒng gè yàng　various
5. 造型　（名）　zàoxíng　model
6. 露怯　lòu qiè　to make a fool of oneself
7. 亭亭玉立　tíngtíng yù lì　tall and straight, slim and graceful
8. 可惜　（形）　kěxī　regretful
9. 安排　（动）　ānpái　arrange
10. 周到　（形）　zhōudào　considerate

注释　Notes

1. 这个景点都被印在纸币上了……

这是一个被动句，用介词"被"来表示被动的动词谓语句称为"被"字句，它说明人或事物受到某种动作的影响而产生某种结果。

"被" is a preposition used in a passive structure.

基本句式为：the basic pattern is:

主语——被——宾语——谓语动词——其他成分

Subject—被—宾语—Predicate verb—Other elements

词典　　被　小李　　拿　　　　走了。

"被"字句中的主语一定是受事者，可以是人或事物，是谓语动词动作的接受对象。

The subject of a "被"－sentence must be the recipient of an action, which can be a person, a thing or an event.

"被"的宾语在意义上是动作的发出者（施事者），有时可以省略。

The object of "被" is actually the doer of the action, which can be omitted sometimes.

例如：这个景点都被印在纸币上了。

　　　　门被吹开了。

"被"字句中的谓语动词一定是及物的，一般是能支配或影响句中主语（受事者）的。

In the "被"—sentence, the predicate verb must be transitive.

例如：我的自行车被他弟弟骑走了。

"被"字句中的谓语动词后一定要有其他成分，一般是动态助词"了"、"过"或各种补语。

In the "被"—sentence, there must be other elements after the verb, and generally, they are "了"，"过" or other complements.

否定副词或助动词要放在"被"前。

The negative adverbs or auxiliary verbs should be put in front of "被".

例如：他没（有）被爸爸打过。

　　　你这样做不好，会被人发现。

2. 我想起来了。

这里"起来"用在动词后表示"想"这一动作完成并达到了目的。

"起来" is placed after the verb, expressing the idea that the action "想" has completed and reached its aim.

例如：学校的书画俱乐部建立起来了。

3. 这个"瀛"字可够难写的!

"够"，副词，表示程度很高。

"够"，an adverb, is used to show a high degree.

例如：商店里的商品可够丰富的。

4. 这个名字起得真有意思。

"起"，动词，宾语为"名字"，"起名字"即给人或事物一个名称。

"起"，a verb, "起名字" means to "name someone" or "give someone a name".

例如：你给你的孩子起个什么名字？

5. 游西湖哪能不坐船呢？

"哪"，副词，用于反问，表示否定，使整个句子的意思变成肯定，即游西湖一定要坐船。

"哪"，an adverb, is used in a rhetorical question to show negation. Therefore, in this sentence the meaning becomes affirmative.

例如：这次活动你哪能不参加？

替换练习　Substitution Drills

1. 它是人们想象中　神奇、美丽　　　　　　　　的理想世界。
　　　　　　　　　　没有战争、没有灾难
　　　　　　　　　　和平、安乐
　　　　　　　　　　富裕、幸福

2. 她　　安排　　得可真周到。
　　　　考虑
　　　　计划
　　　　照顾

会话　Conversations

完成下列会话 Complete the following dialogues
（如括号里有词语或提示，请按要求做 Use words or expressions given in the brackets）

A：这里的水果多吗？
B：很多，各种各样的水果都有。
A：便宜吗？
B：＿＿＿＿＿＿＿＿＿＿＿＿＿＿＿＿＿＿＿＿，一斤香蕉一块钱。（够）

A：西湖的亭子有什么特点？
B：＿＿＿＿＿＿＿＿＿＿＿＿＿＿＿＿＿。（不仅……而且……）
A：开网亭的名字是怎么来的？
B：＿＿＿＿＿＿＿＿＿＿＿＿＿＿＿＿＿。（和……有关）

杭州

【第七集】

杭州街上

韩　佳：大家好，这里是《快乐中国》，我是快乐的韩佳。

大　牛：我是文雅的大牛。

韩　佳：哎，大牛，今天天气又不热，你拿把扇子干吗呀？

大　牛：哎，我大牛这么有文化修养，我总要随身携带一些有品位的东西①。你看，中国的书法和水墨画，大家都比较熟悉。

韩　佳：嗯，说得没错。

大　牛：但是我发现水墨画和书法，都离不了一个东西，那就是印。啊，中国的文化真是源远流长啊！

Zhōngguó de wénhuà zhēn shì yuán yuǎn liú cháng!
中国　的 文化 真 是 源 远 流 长！
China has a culture honoured by centuries.

韩　佳：你到底想说什么呀②？

大　牛：我大牛今天要带大家去一个地方，这个地方被称作是——中国印学博物馆。哎，在哪儿啊？

韩　佳：还是跟我走吧！

大　牛：这边！

Han Jia: Hey, Daniel, it is not hot today. Why are you holding a fan?

Daniel: Hey, I am so well educated that I always have something with me to show my taste. Look, people are familiar with Chinese calligraphy and ink-wash paintings.

Han Jia: Right.

Daniel: I found that neither ink-wash paintings nor calligraphy can do without one thing. That is the seal. Chinese culture does have a very long history.

Han Jia: What are you up to?

Daniel: I am going to take you to a place today. It is called the Seal Museum of China. Hey, where is it?

Han Jia: Follow me.

Daniel: This way.

西泠印社拱门口

大　牛：啊，西泠（líng）印社！

韩　佳：嘘——小声点儿，真丢人！到了这儿还念错字！哎，你这有
　　　　文化的人再好好看看！

大　牛：韩佳，你不会真以为我不认识这个字吧！怎么说我大牛也是
　　　　学中文的人啊！这叫西泠（líng）印社，行吧？

韩　佳：嗯，这回念对了！西泠印社的"泠"和冷热的"冷"两个字
　　　　的偏旁一个是三点水、一个是两点水，所以非常容易搞错。

大　牛：它之所以叫西泠印社，是因为它建在西泠桥的附近③，和温
　　　　度毫无关系。

韩　佳：哎，看来这大牛真是早有准备。佩服，佩服！

大　牛：谢谢！我是昨天晚上才刚查了词典。走吧！

Daniel: Wow, Xileng Seal-engraving Society.

Han Jia: Keep your voice down. You read a character wrong. Hey, you are well educated. Take a closer look at it.

Daniel: Han Jia, do you really think I don't know the character? I am a Chinese learner after all. It is called Xiling Seal-engraving Society.

Han Jia: Right. You got it right this time. "Ling" in Xiling Seal-engraving Society and "leng" in "leng re" have different character component. One has three dots, and the other has two dots. It is easy to get confused.

Daniel: It is called Xiling Seal-engraving Society because it was built near Xiling Bridge. It has nothing to do with temperature.

Han Jia: Hey, it seems that Daniel is well prepared. Great, great.

Daniel: Thank you. I looked it up in the dictionary last night. Come on.

碑刻长廊

韩 佳：这印学可是中华民族的一门传统艺术。

大 牛：没错，好像北京2008年奥运会的会徽，也做成了印章的样子。
我在北京的时候，也经常刻几颗印章什么的。

韩 佳：哎，错了！

大 牛：刻几颗印章，怎么错了？回头我也给你刻几张。

韩 佳：又错了！我们说印章的时候，通常用量词"枚"，一枚印章。

大 牛：哦，原来是我的量词用错了④。*说印章的时候通常用量词
"枚"，一枚印章。*

韩 佳：哎，大牛，正好我这儿有两枚印章，那就麻烦你全都给刻了，
谢谢啊！

大 牛：我哪儿会呀，又得花钱找人帮忙！

Han Jia: Seal engraving is a traditional art of China.

Daniel: Exactly. The emblem of Beijing 2008 Olympics is in the form of a seal. When I was in Beijing, I often engraved seals.

Han Jia: Hey, you are wrong.

Daniel: What's wrong with engraving seals? I will engrave some for you later.

Han Jia: You are wrong again. When we talk about seals, we usually use the quantifier "mei", "yi mei yinzhang".

Daniel: Oh, it turned out I used the wrong quantifier. The Chinese measure word for seals is "mei". "Yi mei yinzhang", a seal.

Han Jia: Hey, Daniel, I have two seals here. Could you please engrave them for me? Thank you.

Daniel: I can't. I will have to pay somebody to do it.

大 牛：哎，韩佳，*那位老人是谁呀？*

韩 佳：这是丁敬的坐像。丁敬是中国印学方面的大师，好多文人都
　　　　非常佩服他。

Hǎoduō wénrén dōu fēicháng pèifú tā.

好多 文人 都 非常 佩服 他。

Many scholars really admire him.

大 牛：哎，对了，韩佳，一提起印章，我常听别人说"篆刻"⑤，
　　　　它到底是什么意思呀？

韩 佳：哦，"篆刻"就是指刻印章。中国古代有一种字体叫作"篆体"，
　　　　而印章上面刻的字呢，往往都是篆体，所以我们把刻印章又
　　　　统称为"篆刻"。

大 牛：哦，这下我明白了！

Daniel: Hey, Han Jia. Who's that old man?

Han Jia: This is the sitting statue of Ding Jing. Ding Jing was a seal master in China. Many scholars admire him very much.

Daniel: Hey, Han Jia. Talking about seals, I often hear people say "zhuanke". What on earth does it mean?

Han Jia: Well, "zhuanke" means seal cutting. There was a kind of character style called "zhuan" in ancient China. The characters on seals are usually zhuan style. So we call seal cutting "zhuanke".

Daniel: Oh, I see.

观乐楼

大　牛：哎，那楼上写的是"乐观"两个字吧？哎，你笑什么？

韩　佳：没什么。哎，你知道"乐观"是什么意思吗？

大　牛：这可难不住我！"乐观"是一个形容词，形容像我一样的人，
　　　　就是精神愉快。

韩　佳：嗯，大牛说得没错。"乐观"是指精神愉快，对事物的发展
　　　　充满信心。哎，大牛，不过这可不是什么"乐观楼"啊！

大　牛：哦，这里应该念"观乐（yuè）楼"，中国古代很多牌匾都是从
　　　　右往左念的。这只是我一时糊涂啊，以后肯定不会出错了。

Daniel: Hey, is the inscription on the building "leguan"? Hey, what are you laughing at?

Han Jia: Nothing. Hey, do you know what "leguan" means?

Daniel: It is easy. "Leguan" is an adjective used to describe people like me, meaning optimistic.

Han Jia: Well, Daniel is right. "Leguan" means optimistic, confident of the progress. Hey, Daniel, but this is not Leguan Building.

Daniel: Well, then it should be called Guanyue Building. Many tablets in ancient China were read from right to left. I was just confused. I won't make the mistake any more.

文澜阁

大 牛：哎，韩佳，这里就是文澜阁，我听说这里藏有《四库全书》。
　　　　你看过吗？

韩 佳：你看过吗？

大 牛：没看过原本。

韩 佳：我在小学的时候，就知道《四库全书》了。它可是中国历史
　　　　上编纂规模最大的一部丛书。

大 牛：嗯，我也知道。它写成以后分抄七部，藏到中国的七大藏书
　　　　阁里了。

韩 佳：对，我们现在看到的这个文澜阁就是中国七大藏书阁之一⑥。

Wénlán Gé shì Zhōngguó qī dà cángshūgé zhī yī.
文澜 阁 是 中国 七 大 藏书阁 之 一。

Wenlan Mansion is home to one of China's seven largest book collections.

文澜阁外

大 牛：逛了西泠印社又去了中国七大藏书阁之一的文澜阁，今天我
　　　　可长了不少见识。不过，韩佳，这些印章还是还给你，自己
　　　　学着刻才有乐趣嘛，对吧！

韩 佳：这个大牛！

Daniel: Hey, Han Jia. This is Wenlan Mansion. I heard that the Complete Collection of Four Treasures is kept here. Have you ever read it?

Han Jia: Have you ever read it?

Daniel: I've never read the original.

Han Jia: When I was in elementary school, I heard about the Complete Collection of Four Treasures. It is the series with the largest editing scale in Chinese history.

Daniel: Well, I know. After it was finished, it was made into seven copies and kept in the seven largest libraries in China.

Han Jia: Right. Wenlan Mansion is one of the seven largest libraries of China.

Daniel: Having visited Xiling Seal-engraving Society and the Wenlan Mansion, one of the seven largest libraries in China, I really learned a lot today. But, Han Jia, I'd better return the seals to you. It is fun only if you learn to carve the seals yourself, isn't it?

Han Jia: Daniel!

生词　Words and Expressions

1. 文雅　　（形）　　wényǎ　　　　　　　　elegant
2. 修养　　（名）　　xiūyǎng　　　　　　　accomplishment
3. 品位　　（名）　　pǐnwèi　　　　　　　　taste
4. 水墨画　（名）　　shuǐmòhuà　　　　　　ink and wash painting
5. 源远流长　　　　　yuán yuǎn liú cháng　to have a long history
6. 传统　　（名）　　chuántǒng　　　　　　tradition
7. 印章　　（名）　　yìnzhāng　　　　　　　seal
8. 文人　　（名）　　wénrén　　　　　　　　man of letters
9. 佩服　　（动）　　pèifú　　　　　　　　　to admire

注释　Notes

1. 我**总**要随身携带一些有品位的东西。

"总"，副词，表示"一直"、"一向"。

"总"，an adverb，means "always".

例如：每次进城我总要到书店去看看。

2. 你**到底**想说什么呀？

"到底"，副词，用在疑问句中，表示进一步追问。

"到底"，an adverb，used in a question to show further enquiry. The sentence means "what on earth do you want to say？".

例如：北京的夏天到底热不热呀？

3. 它**之所以**叫西泠印社，**是因为**它建在西泠桥附近。

"……之所以……是因为……"这一结构主要用来突出说明原因。

"……之所以……是因为……" is similar to "the reason why... is because".

例如：我之所以不参加这次活动，是因为这样的活动没有什么意义。

4. **原来**是我的量词用错了。

"原来"，副词，表示发现以前不知道的情况，含有恍然醒悟的意思。

"原来", an adverb, is used to mean "it turns out...".

例如：我以为他会汉语呢，原来他不会呀。

5. 一提起印章，我常听别人说篆刻……

动词前加"一"表示经过某一短暂动作就得出某种结果。

When "一" is added in front of a verb, it means "once...".

例如：一说到杭州，我就想起西湖的美丽景色。

6. 我们现在看到的这个文澜阁就是中国七大藏书阁之一。

"之一"，意思是"其中的一个"。

"之一" means "one of the...".

例如：西湖是中国有名的旅游风景区之一。

替换练习　Substitution Drills

1.

中国	的	文化	真是	源远流长。
杭州		西湖		景色秀丽
北京		烤鸭		味道鲜美
超市		商品		品种丰富

2.

好多	文人	都非常	佩服他。
	学生		喜欢那位老师
	青年		喜欢那种工作
	农民		了解市场情况

3.

文澜阁	是中国	七大藏书阁	之一。
西施		古代的四大美女	
火药		古代的四大发明	
佛教		三大宗教	

会话　Conversations

完成下列会话 Complete the following dialogues
（如括号里有词语或提示，请按要求做 Use words or expressions given in the brackets）

A：九点了，_____？（到底）

B：我不想去了。

A：怎么了？

B：我身体不太舒服。

A：你为什么想刻一枚印章？

B：_____。（……之所以……是因为……）

A：我也很喜欢印章，我已经有好几枚了。

B：中国传统文化太有意思了。

110

杭州

【第八集】

杭州街景

大　牛：哎，韩佳，我们今天去向何方？

韩　佳：今天要让你大饱眼福，带你去看看"杭州双绝"之一的"虎
　　　　跑泉"。

猛虎模型前

大　牛：来吧，韩佳，慢一点，这里太滑了！啊！

韩　佳：你小心！

大　牛：这儿真有老虎啊？

韩　佳：怎么样？这简直栩栩如生吧！

大　牛：嗯！

韩　佳：要是猛地一看啊，还以为是真的呢，准得把你吓一跳^①！

大　牛：准得吓我一跳？

韩　佳："准"在这里是副词，表示"一定"的意思。我们可以说：
　　　　他准能来。还可以说：工作准能按时完成。

大　牛：*我知道。不过别人也许害怕，我大牛肯定不怕。*

韩　佳：哦，你那么有信心？

大　牛：你没听说过吗^②？有一句俗语叫作什么"小牛不怕大老虎"。
　　　　对对对，小牛不怕大老虎。

韩　佳：什么？我怎么没听说过？这大牛肯定又说错了。

Daniel: Hey, Han Jia. Where are we going today?

Han Jia: Today I'll let you see something rare and fabulous. I am going to take you to visit one of the two unique things of Hangzhou, the Tiger Spring.

Daniel: Come on. Han Jia, walk carefully. It is quite slippery.

Han Jia: Be careful.

Daniel: Is it a real tiger?

Han Jia: It is so lively.

Daniel: Right.

Han Jia: You would think it is a real tiger if you take a quick glance. You would certainly be scared.

Daniel: I would certainly be scared.

Han Jia: "Zhun" is an adverb here, meaning certainly. We can say, "he will certainly come". We can also say, "the work can certainly be finished on time".

Daniel: I see. Maybe other people will be scared, but I will certainly not.

Han Jia: Well, you are so confident.

Daniel: Have you ever heard of an old saying? Calves are not afraid of big tigers. Right. Calves are not afraid of big tigers.

Han Jia: But why haven't I ever heard of it? Daniel must be wrong again.

韩 佳：哎，大牛，你刚才说的那句俗语是什么来着？

大 牛：那个，就是什么"小牛不怕大老虎"。

韩 佳：得了得了③，我知道了。你想说"初生牛犊不怕虎"，对吧？

Chū shēng niúdú bú pà hǔ.

初 生 牛 犊 不 怕 虎。

Young people are daring and dauntless.

大 牛："初生牛犊不怕虎"，就是小牛不怕老虎，形容年轻人非常勇敢，敢于做任何事情。初生牛犊不怕虎，说的就是我大牛！

韩 佳：你就别得意了！看过了虎，这一下我们要去看泉啦。

大 牛：哦，走！

Han Jia: Hey, Daniel, what is the old saying you just mentioned?

Daniel: Calves are not afraid of big tigers.

Han Jia: Well, I see. You mean "chu sheng niudu bu pa hu"?

Daniel: "Chu sheng niudu bu pa hu" literally means that a new born calf is not afraid of tigers. It's used to describe the fact that young people are brave and courageous. They're afraid of nothing and dare to do anything. "Chu sheng niudu bu pa hu" refers to Daniel.

Han Jia: All right. Don't be complacent. We have seen the tiger. Next, we are going to see the spring.

Daniel: All right. Let's go.

场景 Scene　泉 眼

大　牛：这水可真清澈啊！

韩　佳：是啊，这儿的泉水不光看起来清澈透亮，而且喝起来呀……④

大　牛：我尝尝就知道了。

韩　佳：怎么样？

大　牛：又甜又凉，真不错⑤！哎，韩佳，我刚想起来，这里为什么
　　　　叫"虎跑（pǎo）泉"？是不是这里有很多老虎跑来跑去呀？

韩　佳：我可没有说是"虎跑（pǎo）泉"啊，这里应该念"虎跑（páo）泉"。
　　　　"跑"是个多音字，念第二声的时候，表示刨开、挖的意思。

大　牛：啊？那么说，这里的泉水是老虎用爪子刨出来的？

韩　佳：是不是老虎刨出来的，一会儿你就知道了。

大　牛：这个韩佳，又把我的胃口吊起来了⑥。

Daniel: The water is so clear.

Han Jia: Right. The spring water not only looks clear, but also tastes...

Daniel: I will know once I taste it.

Han Jia: How is it?

Daniel: Sweet and cool. Great. Hey, Han Jia, I just remembered. Why is it called the Tiger Spring? Is it because tigers run around here?

Han Jia: I didn't say it was the Tiger Running Spring. It should be Hu Pao Quan. "Pao" has two pronunciations. When it is the second tone, it means pawing.

Daniel: Well, so it means the spring was pawed out by tigers.

Han Jia: Whether it was pawed out by tigers or not, you will know in a moment.

Daniel: Han Jia, you aroused my curiosity again.

梦虎雕塑

韩　佳：哎，大牛，这雕塑讲的就是"梦虎"的故事。

大　牛：怎么又出来了一个"梦虎"的故事？

韩　佳：是这样的，传说唐朝的时候，有个和尚想在这里建寺庙，但是这里缺水缺得厉害。有一天他晚上做梦，梦见神仙告诉他，有老虎刨地的那个地方就有泉水。第二天他醒来，果然发现有两只老虎在那儿刨地。它们刨的那个地方啊，就有一股泉水涌出。

大　牛：哦，这么有趣的传说！这么说，这儿的泉水，也是被神仙指点的呢？

韩　佳：对呀！

大　牛：怪不得这水这么好喝！

Guàibude zhè shuǐ zhème hǎohē!
怪不得　这　水　这么　好喝！

It's no wonder that the water here tastes so great.

Han Jia: Hey, Daniel, the sculpture is about the story of Meng Hu.

Daniel: What's the story of Meng Hu about?

Han Jia: It goes like this. It is said in the Tang Dynasty, a monk wanted to build a temple here. But it was deficient in water. One night, he dreamed that a god told him that a spring would well out where tigers were pawing the ground. When he woke up the next day, he found two tigers were pawing the ground there. And the place they were pawing had a spring coming out.

Daniel: Well, it is an interesting story. Then the spring here was directed by god.

Han Jia: Right.

Daniel: No wonder the water tastes so great.

场景 Scene　　虎跑泉边

大　牛：韩佳，我记得你说了，虎跑泉是"杭州双绝"之一。那另外的一绝呢？

韩　佳：那另外一绝跟虎跑泉有着密切的关系，那就是龙井茶。

大　牛：哦，我明白了。好水沏好茶，好茶更显好水。

韩　佳：嗯，总结得好。等到明天啊，我们好好去品一品龙井茶。

大　牛：明天去啊！干吗今天不去呢？

韩　佳：品龙井茶可是有讲究的。今天来不及了，明天吧。

大　牛：不带我去，我自己去。

Daniel: Han Jia, I remember you said that Tiger Spring was one of the two unique things of Hangzhou. What about the other one?

Han Jia: The other one is closely related to Tiger Spring. It is the Dragon Well Tea.

Daniel: Oh, I see. Nice water makes great tea, and great tea makes even better water.

Han Jia: Well, good summary. Tomorrow we will go and taste the Dragon Well Tea.

Daniel: Tomorrow? Why won't we go today?

Han Jia: There is something special about drinking the Dragon Well Tea. It is too late today. We will go tomorrow.

Daniel: If you don't take me there, I will go by myself.

品茶室内

大　牛：品茶有讲究，我是知道的。不过，凭我大牛的聪明，看看书，
　　　　一会儿就明白了。

韩　佳：大牛，你干吗呢？

大　牛：品茶！哎，韩佳，你要不要欣赏我的茶艺表演？

Nǐ yào bu yào xīnshǎng wǒ de cháyì biǎoyǎn?
你 要 不 要 欣赏 我 的 茶艺 表演？

Would you like to watch my tea culture performance?

韩　佳：你还会茶艺表演？

大　牛：当然了，要不我给你看看①？

韩　佳：好，来！

大　牛：第一步，放茶叶；第二步，倒水；第三步，搅一搅；第四步，
　　　　请喝茶！

韩　佳：哪有你那么喝茶的呀！

大　牛：又错了？

韩　佳：好了好了！这样吧，明天给你请一个真正的茶道高手，给你
　　　　指点一下，让你也品一品正宗的龙井茶。

大　牛：好，让我们期待明天的好水好茶吧！

Daniel: I know there is something special about drinking tea, but as I am so smart, I will understand it once I read some books.

Han Jia: Daniel, what are you doing?

Daniel: Drinking tea. Hey, Han Jia. Would you like to watch my tea culture performance?

Han Jia: You know tea culture performance?

Daniel: Of course. I will show you.

Han Jia: OK. Come on.

Daniel: First, put the tea in. Second, pour the water in. Third, mix them. Fourth, please enjoy yourself.

Han Jia: Who drinks tea as you do?

Daniel: Am I wrong again?

Han Jia: All right. Tomorrow, I will invite a real tea culture master to teach you. You will be able to drink the genuine Dragon Well Tea.

Daniel: OK. Let's look forward to tomorrow's nice water and great tea.

生词　Words and Expressions

1. 栩栩如生　　　　　xǔxǔ rú shēng　　　lifelike
2. 准　　（形、副）　zhǔn　　　　　　　bound; definitely
3. 泉水　（名）　　　quánshuǐ　　　　　spring water
4. 清澈　（形）　　　qīngchè　　　　　　clear
5. 刨　　（动）　　　páo　　　　　　　　to dig, to paw
6. 吊胃口　　　　　　diào wèikǒu　　　　to arouse interest
7. 讲究　（形、动）　jiǎngjiu　　　　　　to be particular about
8. 茶道　（名）　　　chádào　　　　　　　tea rite
9. 期待　（动）　　　qīdài　　　　　　　to expect

注释　Notes

1. 准得把你吓一跳！

"准"，副词，"一定"的意思，用于口语。

"准"，副词，an adverb used in spoken Chinese, means "definitely".

"得（děi）"，这里是助动词，"会"的意思。

"得（děi）"，here an auxiliary verb, means "to be likely".

例如：他要知道杭州这么好玩儿，准得来这儿玩儿几天。

2. 你没听说过吗？

这是用"没……吗"的反问句，起强调肯定作用，表示事实已经如此。

"没……吗" is used to form a rhetorical question, implying that "that is the fact".

例如：我没告诉你吗？那个景点太有意思了，一定要去看。

3. 得了得了，我知道了。

"得了得了"，这里的意思是"算了"，含有不太耐烦的意味。

"得了得了" means here "all right, all right" or "come on, come on", showing a little impatience.

例如：得了得了，大家都别吵了。

4. 这儿的泉水不光看起来清澈透亮，而且喝起来呀……

"不光"，口语词，"不但"的意思。和"而且"配合构成"不光……而且……"句式，表示除前面所说的意思以外，还有更进一层的意思。

"不光……而且……" is similar to "not only... but also...". "不光" is a colloquial word meaning "不但".

例如：这次来杭州不光游览了西湖景区，而且还看望了几位多年不见的老朋友。

5. 又甜又凉，真不错!

"又……又……"这一结构表示两个动作或两种性质、情况都有。

"又……又……" is similar to the structure "both... and...".

例如：这种水果又贵又不好吃，别买了。

6. 又把我的胃口吊起来了。

"吊"，动词，宾语为"胃口"，"吊胃口"指激发起食欲，也比喻激发起对某事的兴趣。

"吊", a verb, used together with its object "胃口", means "to arouse one's appetite", which is a metaphor of arousing one's interest.

例如：听了他对滑雪的介绍，我的胃口被吊起来了，真想去那里滑雪。

7. 要不我给你看看?

"要不"，连词，意思是"如果不这样"。

"要不", a conjunction, means "otherwise..." or "or else...".

例如：给他打个电话吧，要不他会着急。

替换练习 Substitution Drills

1. 怪不得　　　这水这么好喝！
　　　　　　　他来得这么早
　　　　　　　他这么高兴
　　　　　　　今天坐车的人这么多

· ·

2. 你要不要欣赏　　我的茶艺表演？
　　　　　　　　　他画的画儿
　　　　　　　　　王老师写的几首诗
　　　　　　　　　她的钢琴演奏

会话 Conversations

完成下列会话 Complete the following dialogues
（如括号里有词语或提示，请按要求做 Use words or expressions given in the brackets）

A：这虎跑泉的泉水怎么样？
B：太好喝了，_____。（又……又……）
A：听说这虎跑泉还有一个传说故事呢。
B：一会儿请导游讲讲。

· ·

A：明天晚上这儿有一个舞会，他们能来吗？
B：_____。（准）
A：你怎么知道？
B：他们很喜欢跳舞，肯定会来。

杭州

【第九集】

杭州街景

大　牛：快乐的大牛向您问好！

韩　佳：哎，大牛，在杭州你待了这么多天了，你觉得杭州什么最
　　　　多啊？

大　牛：*好多的山，好多的湖，还有桥和塔。你瞧，咱们都看过雷峰塔、*
　　　　宝俶塔，还有灵隐寺的双塔。

韩　佳：那好，今天我再带你去看一座塔——六和塔，它可是西湖古
　　　　塔之首①。快走！

大　牛：*快走！*

Daniel: I am happy Daniel. Hello!

Han Jia: Hey, Daniel, you have been in Hangzhou for several days. What do you think Hangzhou has the most?

Daniel: Well, there are lots of hills, lots of lakes, lots of bridges and lots of pagodas. Look, we have seen Leifeng Pagoda, Baochu Pagoda as well as the Twin Pagodas in Lingyin Temple.

Han Jia: All right. Today I will take you to see another pagoda, Liuhe Pagoda. It is the best ancient pagoda at the West Lake. Come on.

Daniel: Let's go.

韩　佳：大牛，这就是六和塔。

大　牛：哇，真雄伟啊！

韩　佳：嗯，这塔是阁楼式的，这是中国古塔中最常见的一种形式。

Zhè shì Zhōngguó gǔ tǎ zhōng zuì cháng jiàn de yì zhǒng xíngshì.
这 是 中国 古塔中 最 常 见 的一 种 形式。

This is the most common form of ancient Chinese towers.

大　牛：*哎，韩佳，那座雕像是谁？看起来像哪吒！*

韩　佳：这可不是哪吒，他叫"六和"。传说古时候呢，钱塘江里住着一位性情暴躁的龙王，经常用潮水淹没两岸百姓的房子，所以这个六和就带领大众，用石块填江来镇住这个龙王。

大　牛：哦，原来"六和"是个人名啊！六和镇江，真是个小英雄！

韩　佳：但是这只不过是一个传说②。不过这六和塔还真的是北宋的时候，吴越王为了镇住钱塘江的江潮而建的。

大　牛：那六和塔挡住江潮了吗？

韩　佳：建塔镇江啊，只是人们的一个愿望。但是六和塔倒真的给杭州西湖增添了一道新的风景③，而且便利了航运。

大　牛：六和塔和航运有什么关系呢？

韩　佳：你想啊，六和塔雄踞在江边，那么来往的船只呢远远地就能看到它。

大　牛：*我知道了，相当于灯塔④。*

韩　佳：是啊，有了六和塔这个标志，那么船只就不会迷失方向了。

大　牛：嗯，那我们赶快去看看吧！

Han Jia: Daniel. This is Liuhe Pagoda.

Daniel: Wow, how imposing!

Han Jia: Right. It is a multi-storeyed pagoda. It is of the most common style of ancient Chinese pagodas.

Daniel: Hey, Han Jia. Who's that child? He looks like Nezha.

Han Jia: He is not Nezha. He is Liuhe. It is said that in ancient times, in the Qiantang River lived an irascible dragon king. He often flooded people's houses on the banks with tides. So Liuhe led people to fill the river with stones to threaten the dragon king.

Daniel: Well, so Liuhe is a person's name. Liuhe brought the river under control. He was really a young hero.

Han Jia: It is only a tale. But in fact, Liuhe Pagoda was built in Northern Song Dynasty by King Wuyue to bring the tides of the Qiantang River under control.

Daniel: Did Liuhe Pagoda stop the tides?

Han Jia: It's only the wish of people to bring the tides under control by building a Pagoda. But Liuhe Pagoda has indeed added a new view to Hangzhou West Lake. In addition, it has facilitated river transportation.

Daniel: Does Liuhe Pagoda have anything to do with river transportation?

Han Jia: Think about it. Liuhe Pagoda stands high by the river. The boats passing by can see it from distance.

Daniel: Oh, I know. It's like a light house.

Han Jia: Right. With the help of Liuhe Pagoda, boats wouldn't get lost.

Daniel: Yes. Let's go quickly and take a look.

六和塔上

大　牛：哎，韩佳，你好像有一点儿累了吧！

韩　佳：爬这个可比爬七层楼累多了⑤。不过我有决心，肯定不会比你慢。

大　牛：哎呀，要承认自己的不足嘛，不要逞能啊！

韩　佳：哎，你还会说"逞能"这个词儿！

大　牛："逞能"啊，不就是跟你学的嘛！它的意思就是显示出自己有能耐、有本事。

韩　佳：说得没错！

大　牛：哎，韩佳，你看，这外边还挂着铃铛呢！

韩　佳：这座塔每一个檐角上都有铃铛。

大　牛：哦？

韩　佳：哎，大牛，你能帮我算算这座塔上一共有多少个铃铛吗？

Nǐ néng bāng wǒ suànsuan tǎ shàng yǒu duōshao ge língdāng ma?
你 能 帮 我 算算 塔 上 有 多少 个 铃铛 吗？

Can you help me to figure out how many bells the tower has altogether?

大　牛：这还不简单，⑥好，给你算算！每层有七个角，一共有十三层，十三乘以七……哎，韩佳，你等我算完再爬嘛！

Daniel: Hey, Han Jia. You seem to be a little tired.

Han Jia: It is much more tiring than climbing seven floors. But I am confident that I won't fall behind you.

Daniel: Hey, you should admit your limitations. Don't try to.

Han Jia: Hey, you even know the word "cheng neng".

Daniel: I learned it from you. It means to show off one's talent and competence.

Han Jia: Right.

Daniel: Hey, Han Jia, look, there are bells hanging on outside.

Han Jia: There is a bell hanging on each eave of the pagoda.

Daniel: Really?

Han Jia: Hey, Daniel, could you please help me count the number of the bells on the pagoda?

Daniel: It's simple. OK. I will do the calculation for you. There are seven eaves on each storey. There are 13 stories in total. 13 times 7... Hey, Han Jia, don't climb the pagoda before I finish the calculation.

六和塔塔顶

大　牛：啊，塔顶上感觉真凉快啊！

韩　佳：嗯，登上了塔顶才能看得更远。哎，大牛，那儿就是钱塘江了。

大　牛：那么，那就是钱塘江大桥吧？

韩　佳：对呀！

大　牛：哎，韩佳。

韩　佳：嗯？

大　牛：爬过了号称西湖古塔之首的六和塔，我们好像已经把杭州的塔看得差不多了吧！

韩　佳：怎么可能！还有好多塔你都没看着呢！

大　牛：啊，还有？

韩　佳：是啊，杭州城真是古塔荟萃。

Hángzhōu Chéng zhēn shì gǔ tǎ huìcuì.

杭州　城　真是古塔荟萃。

Hangzhou really has an excellent collection of ancient towers.

Daniel: Wow, it feels so cool on the top of the pagoda.

Han Jia: Yes. You can see farther only if you climb up to the top of the pagoda. Hey, Daniel, that is the Qiantang River over there.

Daniel: Then is that the Qiantang River Bridge?

Han Jia: Exactly.

Daniel: Hey, Han Jia.

Han Jia: Yes?

Daniel: After having climbed Liuhe Pagoda, the best ancient pagoda of the West Lake, it seems that we have almost visited all the pagodas in Hangzhou.

Han Jia: How is it possible? There are many more pagodas that you have not seen.

Daniel: Oh, Are there even more?

Han Jia: Yes. Hangzhou really has a larger number of ancient pagodas.

杭
州

大　牛：古塔荟什么？

韩　佳：荟萃啊！"荟萃"就是指有好多英俊的人物或者精美的东西汇集到了一起。比如说："古塔荟萃"，就是说有好多的古塔汇集到了一起。再比如说："群英荟萃"，就是说有很多优秀的人物汇集到了一起。

大　牛：哦，我知道了，"荟萃"就是好多出色的人和美好的东西汇集到一起。例如，"古塔荟萃"就是好多的古塔汇集在一起。你看，我跟韩佳是群英荟萃。

韩　佳：谁说的，你又在乱说了！两个人太少了，不能说荟萃。

大　牛：那好吧，说我们的观众，你们都是群英荟萃。

韩　佳：好吧。

大　牛：哎，我们的节目很快要结束了⑦。

韩　佳：对呀，但是别忘了我们后面的"赏心悦目"！

Daniel: What is it?

Han Jia: "Huicui". "Huicui" means many excellent people or exquisite articles gather together. For example, "gu ta huicui" means many ancient pagodas are erected here. Another example, "qunying huicui", meaning many excellent people gathered together.

Daniel: Oh, I see. "Huicui" means a collection of wonderful things or a group of outstanding people. "Gu ta huicui" means a collection of ancient towers. Look, Han Jia and I are "qunying huicui".

Han Jia: No. You used the wrong word. Only two persons cannot be described as "huicui".

Daniel: All right. What about our audience? You are all excellent people gathering together.

Han Jia: OK.

Daniel: Hey, it's time for us to wrap up our program.

Han Jia: Right. Don't forget the following Feast for the Eyes.

生词 Words and Expressions

1. 塔	（名）	tǎ	pagoda
2. 雄伟	（形）	xióngwěi	magnificent-looking
3. 形式	（名）	xíngshì	form
4. 标志	（名、动）	biāozhì	mark; to mark
5. 迷失	（动）	míshī	to get lost
6. 逞能		chěng néng	to show off one's ability
7. 能耐	（名）	néngnài	ability
8. 荟萃	（动）	huìcuì	(of something excellent) gather
9. 汇集	（动）	huìjí	to assemble
10. 出色	（形）	chūsè	outstanding

注释 Notes

1. 它可是西湖古塔之首。

"之"，古汉语遗留下来的结构助词，与现代汉语中的"的"相当。

"之"，an auxiliary word handed down from classical Chinese, is equivalent to "的" in modern Chinese.

"首"，有"第一"、"最高"的意思。"古塔之首"就是古塔中最好的,最有名的。

"首" means "prime", "the best". "古塔之首" means "the best of ancient pagodas".

例如：海尔集团是中国家电行业之首。

2. 但是这只不过是一个传说。

"只"和"不过"都是副词。两个词合用，表示除此之外没有别的。

"只" and "不过" both are adverbs, meaning "no more than..." when used together.

例如：他只不过开个玩笑，没有任何恶意。

3. 但是六和塔倒真的给杭州西湖增添了一道新的风景……

"倒"，副词，有多种意义，这里表示转折。

The adverb "倒" has various meanings；here it is used to make a disjunctive clause.

例如：这个城市虽然不大，但生活倒挺方便的。

4. 我知道了，（它）相当于灯塔。

"于"，介词，用在动词后，可以引出动作的对象。

"于"，a preposition，used after a verb to introduce the object of an action.

"相当于……"即"和……相当"。

"相当于……" means "be equivalent to...".

例如：工厂今年的产量相当于去年的两倍。

5. 爬这个可比爬七层楼累多了。

这是用介词"比"的比较句，用于比较两个人或两种事物在性状或程度上的差别。基本句式为：

"比" is an expression used in comparison to indicate the differences between two things in quality or degree.

The basic pattern is:

A——比——B——比较的结果

A——比——B——the result of the comparison

这座塔 比 七层楼　　高。

它的否定式是把否定副词"不"放在"比"之前。

The negative form is "不比"，with "不" put before "比".

例如：今天不比昨天热。

6. 这还不简单……

"还"，副词，用在反问句中，表示反问，有"不应该"的意思。"这还不简单"意思是"这应该很简单"。

"还"，an adverb，is used in a rhetorical sentence，meaning "should not"."这还不简单" means "This should be very simple".

例如：这些作业还不容易，我一会儿就做完了。

7. 我们的节目很快要结束了。

"要……了"这一结构表示某一动作或情况很快将要发生或出现。基本句式为：

"要……了" means an action or a situation is going to happen or appear. Its basic pattern is:

主语——要——谓语动词——宾语——了

Subject—要—Predicate verb—Object—了

汽车　　要　　进　　　　站　　了。

我们　　要　　吃　　　　饭　　了。

为了强调时间紧迫，还可以在"要"前加副词"就"、"快"，也可以只用"快……了"。

In order to stress urgency, "就" or "快" may be added in front of "要"; or just use "快……了".

例如：他们就要休息了。

商店快要开门了。

我们快回国了。

"要……了"、"就要……了"前面可加表示具体时间的词语做状语，"快要……了"和"快……了"不能加。

In front of "要……了" or "就要……了", words expressing time as adverbials can be added, but not in front of "快要……了" or "快……了".

例如：九点半飞机要起飞了。

我们明天就要去旅行了。

否定式常用"还没（有）……呢"。

"还没（有）……呢" is often used to make the negative form.

例如：他们还没来呢。

替换练习　Substitution Drills

1. 这是　　　中国古塔　　　中最常见的一种　　　形式。
　　　　　　世界贸易　　　　　　　　　　　　方式
　　　　　　中国自行车　　　　　　　　　　　型号
　　　　　　目前家具　　　　　　　　　　　　款式

2. 你能帮我　算算塔上　　有多少个　铃铛　吗?
　　　　　　数数筐里　　　　　　　鸡蛋
　　　　　　看看屋里　　　　　　　客人
　　　　　　点点仓库里　　　　　　纸箱

3. 杭州城　　　真是　　古塔荟萃。
　　中国的发展　　　　日新月异
　　西湖的景色　　　　名不虚传
　　北京的十月　　　　天高气爽

会话　Conversations

完成下列会话 Complete the following dialogues
（如括号里有词语或提示，请按要求做 Use words or expressions given in the brackets）

A：你们这次爬六和塔了吗?
B：爬了。
A：谁快?
B：＿＿＿＿＿＿＿＿＿＿＿＿＿＿＿＿。（比）

A：听说六和塔和航运有关系，是吗?
B：是呀。
A：什么关系呢?
B：＿＿＿＿＿＿＿＿＿＿＿＿＿＿＿＿。（相当于）

杭州
【第十集】

"碧血丹心" 牌坊

大　牛：大家好，这里是《快乐中国》，我是快乐的韩佳。

韩　佳：我是快乐的大牛……你怎么一上来就捣乱①？该罚！

大　牛：啊，为什么要罚我？这里是《快乐中国》，一直是快快乐乐的嘛！

韩　佳：对呀，快乐是没错，可是今天我们要去的这个地方，是一个非常严肃的地方。

大　牛：非常严肃？哪里呀？

韩　佳：穿过这座牌坊就到了，来吧！

岳王庙门楼前

大　牛："三十功名尘与土，"

韩　佳："八千里路云和月。"哎，大牛，这是著名的《满江红》，描写的是作者热爱祖国、报效祖国的雄心壮志。

大　牛：《满江红》，我上学的时候学过，还唱过呢。是谁写的来着？

韩　佳：哎，跟我进去看看，你不就知道了吗②？

Daniel: Hello, everyone! Welcome to Happy China. I am happy Han Jia.

Han Jia: I am happy Daniel... Why are you making trouble as soon as the show started? You should be punished.

Daniel: Well, why should I be punished? It's Happy China. We are always happy here.

Han Jia: Right. Being happy is not wrong. But today we are going to a very solemn place.

Daniel: Very solemn? Where is it?

Han Jia: It's right behind the memorial archway. Come on.

Daniel: Thirty years, rank and honour, just so much dust.

Han Jia: Eight hundred leagues, travelling with the moon and clouds. Hey, Daniel, this is the famous "Man Jiang Hong". It depicts the writer's devotion to the country and his great ambition to serve the country.

Daniel: Man Jiang Hong. When I was in school, I learned it and even sang it. Who wrote it?

Han Jia: Hey, follow me inside to take a look. You will find it out.

进入岳王庙门楼

大　牛：哎呀，作者到底是谁？快提醒我一下，我一着急就怎么想也
　　　　想不起来了③。

Wǒ　yì　zháojí　jiù　zěnme　xiǎng　yě　xiǎng　bù　qǐlái　le.
我　一　着急　就　怎么　想　也　想　不　起来　了。

I got in a daze and it completely slipped my mind.

韩　佳：大牛，你看那儿！
大　牛："民族英雄"！哦，对了，我想起来了！作者是一个大英雄，
　　　　他好像是宋朝一个很有名的将领，叫什么来着？
韩　佳：他可是中国历史上著名的民族英雄，他的名字叫……
大　牛：岳飞！
韩　佳：终于想起来了！
大　牛：哎呀，刚才一着急我没想起来。岳飞是中国历史上一位很有
　　　　名的将领，他率领岳家军英勇善战，非常有名。
韩　佳：对了，今天我们来的这座岳王庙，就是专门为纪念这位民族
　　　　英雄而建造的④。岳飞出生在中国历史上国家分裂、连年战
　　　　乱的南宋时期。他呢率领士兵，收复了大片的国土。哎，你
　　　　看！那"还我河山"四个字就是他当年征战的时候写下的⑤。
大　牛：没人愿意看见自己的国土四分五裂。
韩　佳：哎，大牛你跟我过来！

Daniel: Well, who on earth is the writer? Please give me a hint. I am so anxious that I can't recall it no matter how hard I try.

Han Jia: Daniel, look over there.

Daniel: A national hero. Oh, right. I remember. The writer was a great hero. It seems he was a famous general in the Song Dynasty. What was his name?

Han Jia: He was a famous national hero in the Chinese history. His name was...

Daniel: Yue Fei.

Han Jia: You finally remember it.

Daniel: Well, I was so anxious just now that I couldn't recall it. Yue Fei was a very famous general in the Chinese history. He commanded the Yue's troops to fight valiantly against the enemies and was very well known.

Han Jia: Right. The Temple of General Yue Fei was specially built to commemorate this national hero. Yue Fei was born in the war-torn Southern Song Dynasty in China. He commanded his troops to recapture vast span of territory. Hey, look, the four characters "huan wo he shan" were written by him in those years when he fought in battles.

Daniel: No one is willing to see his country split apart by war.

Han Jia: Hey, follow me.

韩　佳：你看这幅壁画！

大　牛：哎，这不是我以前在中国的历史书上看到过的《岳母刺字》的故事吗⑥？

韩　佳：对，岳飞在出征前，他的母亲就在他的背上，用针刺下了四个字"尽忠报国"。

大　牛：伟大的母亲养育了伟大的英雄！

Wěidà de mǔqīn yǎngyùle wěidà de yīngxióng!
伟大 的 母亲 养育了 伟大 的 英雄！

A great mother raised a great hero.

场景 Scene　**精忠柏亭**

大　牛：哎，韩佳！

韩　佳：嗯？

大　牛：你看！这不是为英雄修建的亭子吗？怎么只修建半座？这不是对岳飞的不尊重吗？

韩　佳：这半座亭子在民间是有说法的，当时南宋始终不能统一，所以只有半壁江山。

大　牛：只有一半的江山？

韩　佳："江山"在这里是指国土，"半壁"是指国土不完整。

大　牛：哦，那我知道了，修建半个亭子就是表示南宋时期的国土不完整。

Han Jia: Look at the mural.

Daniel: Hey, is it the story I once read in books of the Chinese history about the story of Mrs. Yue tattooing her son Yue Fei?

Han Jia: Right. Before Yue Fei went for a battle, his mother tattooed four characters "Jin Zhong Bao Guo" on his back.

Daniel: A great mother nurtured a great hero.

Daniel: Hey, Han Jia.

Han Jia: Yes?

Daniel: Look, is it the pavilion dedicated to the hero? Why is there only half of a pavilion? Does it show disrespect for Yue Fei?

Han Jia: There is a story about the half pavilion among people. At that time, the Southern Song Dynasty could not be united, so it only had "banbi jiangshan".

Daniel: Half of the territory?

Han Jia: "Jiangshan" means territory. "Banbi" means territory is not complete.

Daniel: Oh, I see. Constructing half a pavilion is to show the incomplete territory of the Southern Song Dynasty.

韩　佳：嗯，没错！

大　牛：哎，韩佳，你快带我去看一下岳飞墓吧！我想瞻仰一下这位
　　　　大英雄。

韩　佳：好，走吧！

场景 Scene　照　壁

韩　佳：哎，你再来看这四个字，"尽忠报国"。这其中有一个字少了
　　　　一笔。

大　牛：就是这个"国"字吧？恐怕在这里也是表示疆土不完整。

韩　佳：嗯，说得对，可见当时的人民是多么希望祖国统一啊！

Rénmín shì duōme xīwàng zǔguó tǒngyī!
人民　是　多么　希望　祖国　统一！

The people hoped so much that the motherland could be unified.

Han Jia: Right.

Daniel: Hey, Han Jia, take me to look at the Mausoleum of General Yue Fei. I want to show my respect for the great hero.

Han Jia: All right. Come on.

Han Jia: Hey, look at the four characters "Jin Zhong Bao Guo" again. There is one character among them that lacks one stroke.

Daniel: Is it the character "Guo"? I guess it indicates the incomplete territory as well.

Han Jia: Right. It shows that people hoped so much that the motherland could be unified.

岳飞墓门口

大　牛：韩佳，我不懂，为什么岳飞墓的门口跪着四个铁人儿呢？

韩　佳：这四个就是谋害岳飞将军的坏人，他们将永远跪在那里！

大　牛：哎，对，让他们……有一个成语怎么说？

韩　佳："遗臭万年"。

大　牛：对，"遗臭万年"。

韩　佳："遗臭万年"就是说，让坏名声流传下去，永远遭到人们的唾骂。

大　牛：嗯，"遗臭万年"就是让坏名声流传下去。我呢，想做一个流芳万古的人。

韩　佳：哎，大牛，错了！刚才你可以说"遗臭万年"，但是不能说"流芳万古"，一定要说"万古流芳"啊！

大　牛："流芳万古"和"万古流芳"，不都是好名声流传下去吗？差不多。

韩　佳：那可不行，这成语的格式都是固定的，不能随便颠倒顺序，所以一定要说"万古流芳"。

大　牛：那好吧，让我们都做万古流芳的人吧！

韩　佳：嗯，好了，大牛，今天的节目又该结束了。下面呢，再让我们去瞻仰一下这位民族英雄吧！

大　牛：好！

Daniel: Han Jia, I don't know why there are four iron men kneeling in front of the Mausoleum of General Yue Fei.

Han Jia: These four men conspired to murder General Yue Fei. They will kneel here forever.

Daniel: Right. Let them... What is the idiom?

Han Jia: "Yi chou wan nian".

Daniel: Right. "Yi chou wan nian".

Han Jia: "Yi chou wan nian" means leaving a notorious fame in history and being cursed by people forever.

Daniel: Right. "Yi chou wan nian" means to have a bad reputation which is cursed for centuries. I want to "liufang wangu".

Han Jia: Hey, Daniel, you are wrong. you can say "yi chou wan nian". But you cannot say "liufang wangu". You must say "wangu liufang".

Daniel: Both "liufang wangu" and "wangu liufang" mean leaving a good name in history. They are similar.

Han Jia: No. The idioms have fixed patterns. You cannot reverse the order. So we can only say "wangu liufang".

Daniel: All right. Let us leave good fame in history.

Han Jia: All right. Daniel, it's time to wrap up our program. Next, let's go and show our respect for the national hero again.

Daniel: All right.

生词 Words and Expressions

1. 功名	（名）	gōngmíng		fame and position
2. 雄心壮志		xióngxīn zhuàngzhì		ambition
3. 英雄	（名）	yīngxióng		hero
4. 英勇善战		yīngyǒng shànzhàn		brave and skillful in battle
5. 纪念	（动）	jìniàn		to commemorate
6. 四分五裂		sì fēn wǔ liè		to fall apart
7. 统一	（名、动）	tǒngyī		to unify
8. 瞻仰	（动）	zhānyǎng		to pay respect to
9. 祖国	（名）	zǔguó		motherland
10. 流传	（动）	liúchuán		to spread, to circulate

注释 Notes

1. 你怎么一上来就捣乱？

"一……就……"这一结构表示一种动作或情况出现后另一种动作或情况紧接着发生。"一上来"意思是"一开始"。

"一……就……" is similar to "as soon as...", and "一上来" means "at the very beginning".

例如：这场比赛他一上来就得了一分。

2. 跟我进去看看，你不就知道了吗？

"你不就知道了吗？"是个反问句，表示肯定的意思，即"你就知道了"。

"你不就知道了吗？" is a rhetorical question, meaning "you'll know then".

例如：不就告诉他下午三点开会吗？（告诉他下午三点开会。）

3. 我一着急就怎么想也想不起来了。

"怎么"，疑问代词，这里表示不管用什么方式都……

"怎么" means "however" or "in whatever way".

例如：这个汉字太难写了，我怎么写也写不好。

4．今天我们来的这座岳王庙，就是专门为纪念这位民族英雄而建造的。

"为……而……"是一组常用的关联词，"为"，介词，表示后边动作的目的；"而"，连词，把前面表示目的的成分连接到动词上。

In this structure，"为"，is a preposition used to introduce the aim of the following action，and "而" is a conjunction connecting the verb.

例如：大家要为取得优异成绩而努力学习。

5．那"还我河山"四个字就是他当年征战的时候写下的。

"是……的"结构用于强调已经完成的动作发生的时间、地点、方式等。

"是……的" is a structure used to emphasize the time，place or manner of a completed action.

例如：他们是昨天下午来的。（强调时间）

我是在北京出生的。　（强调地点）

他们是坐飞机来的。　（强调方式）

否定式是"不是……的"。

例如：他不是 1983 年出生的。

6．这不是我以前在中国的历史书上看到过的"岳母刺字"的故事吗？

这是一个反问句，"不是……吗"用于强调肯定的意思和语气。

It is a rhetorical question."不是……吗" is used to emphasize the affirmation.

例如：你不是在北京生活过三年吗？给我们介绍一下北京的情况吧。

替换练习　Substitution Drills

1. 我　一　　着急　　　　就　　怎么想也想不起来了。
　　　　　　出门　　　　　　　赶上下雨
　　　　　　感冒　　　　　　　发烧
　　　　　　到杭州　　　　　　去看你

2. 伟大的母亲　　　养育了　　伟大的英雄。
　　长江、黄河　　　　　　　中华民族
　　一个贫穷妇女　　　　　　五个孩子
　　地球　　　　　　　　　　全人类

3. 人民　　　是多么希望　　祖国统一。
　　我　　　　　　　　　　到北京去看看
　　阿里　　　　　　　　　到中国来学习汉语
　　大牛　　　　　　　　　有一天能登上长城

会话　Conversations

完成下列会话　Complete the following dialogues
（如括号里有词语或提示，请按要求做　Use words or expressions given in the brackets）

　　A：岳飞是什么人，你知道吗？
　　B：＿＿＿＿＿＿＿＿＿＿＿＿＿＿＿。（用"怎么"反问）
　　A：岳飞写了一首有名的词，你学过没有？
　　B：＿＿＿＿＿＿＿＿＿＿＿＿＿＿。（不但……而且……）

　　A：岳飞出征前，她母亲在他背上刺了四个字，你知道是哪四个字吗？
　　B：＿＿＿＿＿＿＿＿＿＿＿＿＿＿。（一……就……）
　　A：别着急，你再想想！
　　B：＿＿＿＿＿＿＿＿＿＿＿＿＿＿。（起来）

杭州

【第十一集】

韩　佳：今天啊……哎，您看见大牛了吗？

大　牛："出淤泥而不染"的大牛来了。

韩　佳：张口就来！那你知道这句话什么意思吗？

大　牛：当然知道！它是说，虽然荷花它长在池塘的淤泥里面，但是它不受污泥的污染。

韩　佳：那比喻什么呢？

大　牛：即使环境不好，人也不变坏。

韩　佳：嗯，差不多！哎，大牛，你刚才去哪儿了？半天也没找着你。

大　牛：我知道我们今天来的这个地方叫"曲院风荷"。院子和风都有，可是我找遍了整个河塘，既没有看见一朵荷花，也没有听见什么曲子呀①？

韩　佳：中国四大国花之一的荷花，又被称做"夏荷"。现在已经是秋天了，看不到荷花了。

Xiànzài shì qiūtiān, kàn bu dào héhuā le.
现在 是 秋天，看 不 到 荷花 了。

It's autumn, you won't see any lotus at this time of year.

Han Jia: Today... Hmm, have you seen Daniel?

Daniel: Here comes the incorruptible Daniel.

Han Jia: Well put. But do you know what that phrase means?

Daniel: Of course. It means that though the flowers of lotus grow out of mud in a pond, they aren't dirtied by it.

Han Jia: What does it actually refer to?

Daniel: A person is not tainted by the corrupt environment.

Han Jia: Pretty close. Hey, where were you a moment ago? I was looking for you all over.

Daniel: I know this place is named "Qu Yuan Feng He". We have garden and wind, but I've looked the pond all over and didn't see one single lotus. And, there's no music either.

Han Jia: Lotus, one of the four Chinese national flowers, is also called summer lotus. It's already autumn, you won't see any lotus flowers at this time of the year.

场景 Scene "曲院风荷" 内

大　牛：哎，韩佳，刚才你只讲了一半儿。这个风和院我都知道了，可是演奏曲子的人呢？

韩　佳：说到这里啊，我正好要给你纠正一个读音。这里不读"曲(qǔ)院风荷"，应该说是"曲(qū)院风荷"。

大　牛：哦，不是曲子的"曲"！

韩　佳：对呀！它这里的"曲(qū)"，其实就是代表曲酒。

大　牛：啊，怎么又跟酒联系上了？

韩　佳：简单地说，这里曾经是南宋时期酿制官酒的地方。酿酒的院子里种满了荷花，轻风一来，酒香、花香满院飘香。所以，这里就叫"曲院风荷"。

大　牛：虽然没有人演奏曲子，可是能酿酒也不错。我大牛也有机会尝一尝美酒了！

韩　佳：哎，既然来了，我们正好去看一看中国古代的酿酒技术。

大　牛：好好好，看看我的酒量！

韩　佳：啊？

大　牛：我是说看看好酒怎么酿。

韩　佳：这个大牛。

Daniel: Hey, Han Jia, you are not done with your explanation yet. I already know about the garden and wind, but where are the musicians?

Han Jia: Speaking of this, I'll need to correct your pronunciation here. "Qu" here is not read with the third tone, but the first.

Daniel: Ah, so it's not music.

Han Jia: That's right. "Qu", here, refers to the qu liquor.

Daniel: What does liquor have to do with it?

Han Jia: Briefly speaking, this is where official wine was brewed in the Southern Song Dynasty. The brewery had a garden full of lotus. The scent of wine and flowers filled the air as the wind blew. Thus came the name of "Qu Yuan Feng He".

Daniel: Though no musicians are around, it's nice to have wine brewed here. Daniel has a chance to taste good wine now.

Han Jia: Well, since we're here, we should go to check out the techniques of ancient Chinese brewing.

Daniel: Great! Time to test my alcohol consumption.

Han Jia: What?

Daniel: I mean... let's go to see how wine was brewed.

Han Jia: Daniel... Daniel...

"曲院风荷"院内

韩 佳：酒的酿造也是一门学问。法国的葡萄酒世界闻名，中国古
　　　代的酿酒工艺也非常讲究。十几个步骤，一个步骤都不能
　　　马虎②。要不然，可就酿不出上好的美酒来了！

大 牛：嗯，没想到这酿酒的过程比我想象的要复杂得多。

Niàng jiǔ de guòchéng bǐ wǒ xiǎngxiàng de yào fùzá de duō.
酿 酒 的 过程 比我 想象 的 要 复杂 得 多。

The process of brewing is more complicated than I'd imagined.

"曲院风荷"内

大 牛：哎，韩佳，我是走不动了，你呀接着逛。

韩 佳：真走不动了？

大 牛：嗯，走不动，太累了！

韩 佳：那好吧，你在这儿休息！观众朋友们，我带您去品尝杭州名
　　　菜——西湖醋鱼。

大 牛：啊，韩佳，你一个人吃不完一条鱼吧……

韩 佳：没事儿啊，还有观众朋友们呢。赶紧走吧！

大 牛：来！

Han Jia: Wine brewing is a science of its own. The French wine is world famous. The ancient Chinese art of brewing is also quite exquisite. There are over a dozen steps, none of which can be taken lightly if you want to brew good wine.

Daniel: The process of brewing is much more complicated than I'd imagined.

Daniel: I'm exhausted, Han Jia. Why don't you just go ahead?

Han Jia: Are you sure?

Daniel: I'm totally worn out.

Han Jia: Okay, then. You may rest here. Friends, I'll take you to try a famous Hangzhou dish—the West Lake sour fish.

Daniel: Huh? Han Jia, you can't possibly finish an entire fish alone...

Han Jia: It's okay, I've got all our audience too. Hurry up.

Daniel: Come on!

　郭　庄

大　牛：哎，韩佳，我们现在在哪儿啊？这个地方跟一个花园似的③，
　　　　根本就不像饭馆啊！

韩　佳：你呀怎么就想着吃！这里是西湖的古典园林——郭庄。

大　牛：啊，我们到郭庄来吃西湖醋鱼？

韩　佳：我们是来钓鱼！

大　牛：啊？这鱼还得自己钓啊？哎，韩佳，我们就不能买一条鱼
　　　　吗？干吗非得自己钓啊④？

韩　佳：这你就不懂了吧。吃自己钓上来的鱼，那才有味道呢！这叫
　　　　"自力更生"。

大　牛：啊？什么叫"自力更生"？

韩　佳："自力更生"就是指不依靠外力，只靠自己的力量把事情办好。

大　牛：哦，我知道了。"自力更生"就是靠自己的力量，把事情办好。

zì lì gēng shēng
自 力 更 生

rely on one's own efforts

164

Daniel: Where are we, Han Jia? It looks like a garden here, not a restaurant.

Han Jia: The only thing on your mind is food. This is Guo Zhuang, a classical style garden of the West Lake.

Daniel: We're here to have the West Lake sour fish, aren't we?

Han Jia: We're here to fish!

Daniel: Huh? We have to do the fishing ourselves? Han Jia, can't we just buy a fish? Why bother with fishing?

Han Jia: You don't understand. It tastes better if you do the actual fishing. This is "zi li geng sheng".

Daniel: Hmm? What does that mean?

Han Jia: "Zi li geng sheng" means using one's own efforts to make something happen.

Daniel: Oh, I see. "Zi li geng sheng" means to accomplish something depending completely on one's own efforts.

郭庄鱼塘边

大　牛：哎，韩佳，都这么半天了⑤，什么时候才能钓到鱼啊？

韩　佳：急什么⑥？反正什么时候钓上来什么时候就去吃⑦。钓不到鱼的呀，就饿着！

大　牛：啊？不会吧！

韩　佳：哎，鱼上钩了，上钩了！

大　牛：哎，给我给我！

韩　佳：到"楼外楼"吃西湖醋鱼去喽！

大　牛：好，走喽！

Daniel: Han Jia, it's been forever. When are we going to catch a fish?

Han Jia: Be patient. We'll eat the fish when we catch one. If we don't catch any, we don't eat anything.

Daniel: Are you kidding?

Han Jia: Hey, I've got one!

Daniel: Let me carry it. Let me carry it.

Han Jia: Let's go to "Louwai Lou" to have the West Lake sour fish!

Daniel: Great! Let's go!

韩　佳：大牛，赶紧尝尝吧！

大　牛：好，那我不客气了！……

韩　佳：怎么样？

大　牛：嗯，又鲜又嫩，又甜又酸，感觉还有一点螃蟹的鲜味。

韩　佳：是啊。哎呀，大牛，你都吃饱了，这后面的杭州美食可怎么办啊！

大　牛：啊？还有什么呀？

韩　佳：有宋嫂鱼羹、叫化童子鸡、龙井虾仁、蟹汁桂鱼，还有清汤鱼圆等等。

大　牛：啊？这么多！我的肚子快撑破了。要不下次吧，下次我请客！

韩　佳：哟，这可难得啦。不过别忘了观众朋友们！

大　牛：嗯，忘不了！

Han Jia: Go ahead, Daniel.

Daniel: Don't mind if I do.

Han Jia: How does it taste?

Daniel: Hmm... Fresh and tender. Sweet and sour! It also has the delicious taste of crabs.

Han Jia: Hey, Daniel. Leave some room for more great delicacy!

Daniel: Huh? What else is there?

Han Jia: We've got Songsao Fish Stew, Tongzi Chicken, Longjing Shrimp, Fish with Crab Juice, Fish Ball Soup, and many more...

Daniel: Wow... That many? My stomach is about to burst. How about next time? I'll treat you.

Han Jia: Well, that'll be a first! Don't forget our friends!

Daniel: Of course not.

生词　Words and Expressions

1. 淤泥　（名）　　　yūní　　　　　silt
2. 荷花　（名）　　　héhuā　　　　　lotus
3. 池塘　（名）　　　chítáng　　　　pond
4. 污染　（名、动）　wūrǎn　　　　　pollution; to pollute
5. 环境　（名）　　　huánjìng　　　　environment
6. 酿造　（动）　　　niàngzào　　　　to brew
7. 过程　（名）　　　guòchéng　　　　procedure
8. 复杂　（形）　　　fùzá　　　　　　complicated
9. 自力更生　　　　　zì lì gēng shēng　to rely on one's own effort

注释　Notes

1. 可是我找遍了整个河塘，既没有看见一朵荷花，也没有听见过什么曲子呀。

"既……也……"这一结构连接两个结构相同或相似的词语或短语，后一部分表示进一步补充说明前一部分。

The structure "既……也……" links two similar phrases or expressions with the latter complementing the former.

例如：出去旅游的时候，既要玩儿好，也要休息好。

2. 一个步骤都不能马虎。

"一……都（也）不（没）……"这种结构，表示对某种情况的强烈否定。

The structure "一……都（也）不（没）……" is used to indicate strong negation.

例如：教室里一个人也没有，他们到哪儿去了呢？

3. 这个地方跟一个花园似的……

"跟"，介词；"似的"，助词。"跟……似的"相当于"和……一样"。

The structure "跟……似的" formed by the preposition "跟" and the auxiliary word "似的" is equivalent to "和……一样", meaning "to be like...".

例如：这小伙子真有劲，跟牛似的。

4. 干吗非得自己钓啊？

"干吗"，意思是"为什么"；"非得"，副词，表示"必须"。

"干吗" means "why"."非得", an adverb, means "must".

例如：你干吗不早点来呢？

这机器非得他来才能修好。

5. 都这么半天了……

"都"，副词，意思是"已经"，句末常有"了"。

"都", an adverb, means "already", and "了" is often added to the end of the sentence.

例如：都七点了，他们怎么还不来？

"这么"，代词，表示强调。"这么半天"强调时间长。

"这么", a pronoun, here is used for emphasis on the length of time.

例如：都这么晚了，你不要出去了。

6. 急什么？

这里"什么"用在形容词"急"后面,表示对"急"的否定,意思是"不用着急"、"不必着急"。

"什么" is put after the adjective "急" to negate "急", meaning "don't need to worry".

例如：贵什么？看一次电影才花五块钱。

7. 反正什么时候钓上来什么时候就去吃。

"反正"，副词，表示虽然情况不同但结果并没有区别。

"反正", an adverb, means "anyway".

例如：反正一天到晚他都在家，你什么时候来都可以。

"什么……什么……"，"什么"，疑问代词，句中两个"什么"前后照应，表示前者决定后者。

In the structure, there are two "什么" (interrogative pronoun, meaning "what"), the later situation being determined by the first one.

例如：他什么时候来，咱们什么时候走。

替换练习　Substitution Drills

1. 现在是　秋天，　看不到　荷花　了。
　　　　　春天　　　　　　雪花
　　　　　冬天　　　　　　桃花
　　　　　夏天　　　　　　梅花

- -

2. 酿酒的过程　比我想象的要　复杂　得多。
　　学习汉语　　　　　　　　难
　　这里的条件　　　　　　　好
　　上海的夏天　　　　　　　热

会话　Conversations

完成下列会话 Complete the following dialogues
（如括号里有词语或提示，请按要求做 Use words or expressions given in the brackets）

　　A：他们是美国人还是加拿大人？
　　B：＿＿＿＿＿＿＿＿＿＿＿＿＿＿＿。（既……也……）
　　A：那他们是哪国人呢？
　　B：＿＿＿＿＿＿＿＿＿＿＿＿＿＿＿。

- -

　　A：你喝过茅台酒吗？
　　B：喝过。
　　A：跟你想象的一样吗？
　　B：不一样，＿＿＿＿＿＿＿＿＿＿＿＿＿。（比）

杭州

【第十二集】

新湖滨集贤亭

韩 佳：大牛！

大 牛：哎！

韩 佳：提问！

大 牛：回答！

韩 佳：西湖上一共有几条堤？

大 牛：一共有苏堤、白堤两条堤，有没有其他的堤我得看地图。

韩 佳：别找了，西湖上一共有三条堤：苏堤、白堤，还有杨公堤。

大 牛：哦，杨公堤，这条堤好像是一位姓杨的人修筑的吧①？

韩 佳：嗯，没错啊，他叫杨孟瑛，是明朝时候杭州的知府。他治理
　　　　西湖的时候，用湖里的淤泥堆起了一条长堤。

大 牛：苏堤、白堤我都看过，剩下的这个杨公堤我也不能落（là）下。
　　　　韩佳，咱们赶紧去看看吧！

韩 佳：只可惜啊，清朝以后，西湖的里湖逐渐淤塞，所以杨公堤就
　　　　被废掉了。

大 牛：啊？没有了，那就没的可看了！

韩 佳：不过呢到了 2002 年，杭州市政府启动了西湖综合保护工作，
　　　　不到一年的时间，杨公堤就恢复了它原来的模样。

Yánggōng Dī huīfùle tā yuánlái de múyàng.
杨公　堤　恢复了　它　原来　的　模样。
The Yanggong Causeway has restored its original appearance.

Han Jia: Daniel.

Daniel: Yeah?

Han Jia: Question!

Daniel: Answer!

Han Jia: How many causeways are there over the West Lake?

Daniel: There are the Su and the Bai Causeways; I'll have to check the map for others...

Han Jia: Don't bother with the map. There are a total of three causeways. The Su, the Bai, and the Yanggong Causeways.

Daniel: I see. The Yanggong Causeway must have been built by someone named Yang, right?

Han Jia: Exactly. His name was Yang Mengying. He was the governor of Hangzhou in the Ming Dynasty. When harnessing the West Lake, he used the mud from the lake to construct this causeway.

Daniel: I've already visited the Su and the Bai Causeways, I've got to see the Yanggong causeway as well. Let's hurry up and go, Han Jia.

Han Jia: Unfortunately, the inner West Lake started to become blocked since the Qing Dynasty and the Yanggong Causeway was demolished.

Daniel: What? So we won't get to see it?

Han Jia: However, the Hangzhou government started a comprehensive West Lake protection campaign in 2002. Within a year's time, the Yanggong Causeway was restored to its original form.

茅家埠

韩 佳：大牛，这杨公堤和苏堤啊遥遥相对，也就是说虽然离得很远，但却互相对着②。

大 牛：哎，韩佳，杨公堤有没有苏堤长？苏堤上可是有六座桥呢！

韩 佳：杨公堤可比苏堤长，而且堤上也有六座桥，和苏堤上的六座桥合称为"西湖十二桥"。哎，大牛，提问！

大 牛：回答！

韩 佳：西湖上一共有多少座桥？

大 牛：西湖上一共有十二座桥。这个韩佳，自己刚说完又问我，她的忘性太大了吧！

韩 佳：可不是我忘性大，我刚才说苏堤和杨公堤上一共有十二座桥。要说西湖上的桥啊，那可数不清啦。你看，光这茅家埠就有好几座呢！

大 牛：茅家埠？这又是什么地方啊？

韩 佳：哦，忘了给你介绍了！我们现在在杨公堤附近的茅家埠，这也是前段时间才刚恢复的景观。

大 牛：嗯，这儿的环境真不错！小桥、流水，还有茅草屋，感觉就像一个大花园。

韩 佳：是啊，这里展示了江南水乡的田园风光。

Zhèli zhǎnshìle Jiāngnán shuǐxiāng de tiányuán fēngguāng.
这里 展示了 江南 水乡 的 田园 风光。

This place displays the rural scenery of the south of the River Yangtze.

Han Jia: The Yanggong and the Su Causeways "yaoyao xiang dui", which means that they face each other from a great distance.

Daniel: Hey, Han Jia. Is the Yanggong Causeway longer than the Su Causeway? You know, there are six bridges on the Su Causeway.

Han Jia: It is indeed longer than the Su Causeway and has six bridges as well. Together with the Su Causeway bridges, they are called the Twelve Bridges of the West Lake. Daniel, question!

Daniel: Answer!

Han Jia: How many bridges are there on the West Lake?

Daniel: There are a total of twelve bridges. She just said that a minute ago. There must be something wrong with her memory.

Han Jia: I don't have a memory problem. I only said there were 12 bridges on the Su and the Yanggong Causeways. The number of bridges on the entire the West Lake is countless. You see, there are quite a few here at Maojiabu.

Daniel: Maojiabu? What is it?

Han Jia: Oh, yeah, I forgot to tell you about it. We're now at Maojiabu, which neighbors the Yanggong Causeway. This is also a recently renovated scenic site.

Daniel: I see. The environment here is great. Bowing bridges, flowing water, and thatched huts. Feels like a giant garden.

Han Jia: That's right. This place displays the rural scenery of the south of the Yangtze River.

新湖滨 "送别白居易" 雕塑

大　牛：哎，韩佳，咱们这是走到哪儿了？

韩　佳：这里是新建的湖滨景区，是城区通向西湖的大门。

大　牛：哦，欢迎欢迎！您好您好！

韩　佳：大牛，你知道他是谁吗你就欢迎他！

大　牛：那他是谁呢？

韩　佳：这位老人正在送别白居易。你看，这位就是白居易③。这是
　　　　当时他离开杭州时的情景。

大　牛：哦，原来是老百姓在送老市长！

韩　佳：嗯，白居易为西湖做出了巨大的贡献，老百姓当然爱戴他了！

大　牛：老百姓爱戴？老百姓爱戴什么？爱戴帽子？

韩　佳：哎呀，你又胡说什么呀④？"爱戴"是敬爱拥护的意思，白
　　　　居易深受老百姓的爱戴。

大　牛：哦，"爱戴"就是热爱和拥护的意思。比如说：他深受老百
　　　　姓的爱戴。他深受老百姓的爱戴。白居易也深受我的爱戴。
　　　　谢谢了，好市长！

Daniel: Where are we now, Han Jia?

Han Jia: This is the new lakeside scenic site. It is the gateway to the West Lake from the city.

Daniel: Hey, welcome! How do you do!

Han Jia: Hey, Daniel, do you know who this man is?

Daniel: Um, who is he?

Han Jia: This elderly gentleman is seeing off Bai Juyi. Look, this is Bai Juyi. This is the scene of his leaving Hangzhou.

Daniel: So it's the people seeing off their mayor.

Han Jia: Yes. Bai Juyi made great contributions to the West Lake, so the people really "aidai" him.

Daniel: "Aidai"? Love to wear? What did the people love to wear? Hats?

Han Jia: What are you talking about, Daniel? "Aidai" means to love and respect. Bai Juyi was deeply loved and respected by the people.

Daniel: Oh, "aidai" means to love and respect. For example, "ta shen shou laobaixing de aidai." He is deeply loved and respected by the public. Bai Juyi is also deeply loved and respected by me. Thank you, my good mayor!

新湖滨古杭州地图

大　牛：哇，湖滨景区的新鲜东西还真是不少啊！韩佳，这里怎么还
　　　　会有一张石头做的地图呀⑤？

韩　佳：这是清代的杭州城区地形图。

Zhè shì Qīngdài de Hángzhōu chéngqū dìxíngtú .
这 是 清代 的 杭州 城区 地形图。

This is a map of Hangzhou in the Qing Dynasty.

韩　佳：当时的十座城门和所有的主要街道都在这张地图上标得清
　　　　清楚楚。

大　牛：哦，哎，韩佳，提问！

韩　佳：回答！

大　牛：我也考考你这个杭州人！你能不能在这张地图上，找到你自
　　　　己的家？

韩　佳：我家啊，应该在那儿，对吧？

大　牛：哼，反正我哪儿也不认识，你说在哪儿就在哪儿呗⑥！

韩　佳：哎，真的，我家就在那儿！

Daniel: Wow, there are so many interesting things here at the new lakeside. How come there's a map made of stone here?

Han Jia: This is a map of Hangzhou in the Qing Dynasty.

Han Jia: The ten gates of the city and all the main roads of the time are clearly marked on this map.

Daniel: Hey, Han Jia. Question!

Han Jia: Answer!

Daniel: I've got a question for you, Hangzhou native. Can you locate your house on this map?

Han Jia: My house? It should be over there. Right?

Daniel: Well, I have no idea where's where. So, whatever you say...

Han Jia: Hey, that really is the location of my house!

新湖滨音乐喷泉

韩 佳：怎么样？大牛，带你来看西湖的夜景没白来吧[7]？

大 牛：嗯，没白来！哎，你看这个灯光多好看！

韩 佳：是啊，你看那些水柱，伴随着音乐变换着不同的造型。哎，
大牛，你知道这叫什么吗？

大 牛：我知道，这就是新湖滨的音乐喷泉。*音乐喷泉*。

韩 佳：对，对。好了，观众朋友们，现在就让我们在音乐的陪伴下
再去欣赏一下新西湖、新杭州吧！

Han Jia: What do you think, Daniel? The night scene here is worth our trip, huh?

Daniel: Yes, indeed. The lighting here is so beautiful.

Han Jia: Look at the sprays of water, reshaping to the music. Do you know what it's called, Daniel?

Daniel: Yep. This is the musical fountain of the new Lakeside. The musical fountain.

Han Jia: Yes. That's right. All right, friends. Let's go along with the wonderful music and revisit the new West Lake and the new Hangzhou.

生词 Words and Expressions

1.修筑	(动)	xiūzhù	to build
2.恢复	(动)	huīfù	to recover, to restore
3.模样	(名)	múyàng	appearance
4.展示	(动)	zhǎnshì	to display
5.田园	(名)	tiányuán	countryside
6.风光	(名)	fēngguāng	landscape
7.爱戴	(动)	àidài	to love and admire
8.地形图	(名)	dìxíngtú	relief map
9.造型	(名)	zàoxíng	modelling
10.喷泉	(名)	pēnquán	fountain

注释   Notes

1. 这条堤好像是一位姓杨的人修筑的吧?

"是……的",这个结构除了可以用来强调已经完成的动作发生的时间、地点、方式等以外,有时也可以用来强调施事者。

"是……的", apart from being used to emphasize the time, place or manner of a completed action, can also be used to emphasize the agent.

例如: 这个建议是李先生提出来的。

有关"是……的"请参见本书第十集注⑤。

Please refer to Note 5, Lesson 10 of this volume for the explanation of the structure.

2. 也就是说虽然离得很远,但却互相对着。

"虽然……但……",这是一个表示转折关系的结构。"虽然",连词,表示让步,承认甲事为事实;后一分句常用"但"、"但是"、"却"等词呼应,表示乙事并不因甲事而不成立。

In Chinese, the structure "虽然……但……" is unlike that in English. "虽然"meaning "although" and "但" meaning "but" are used together. "但" can be replaced by "但是","却".

例如：我们虽然已经分别了十多年，但却经常联系。

3. 这位就是白居易。

"就"，副词，这里用来加强肯定意思和语气。

"就"，an adverb，is used to emphasize the affirmation.

例如：我家就在前面那条街上。

4. 你又胡说什么呀？

"胡说"，动词，指没有根据地随意乱说。

"胡说"，a verb，means "to speak without ground".

例如：你别听他胡说了，事情根本不是这样的。

5. 这里怎么还会有一张石头做的地图呀？

"怎么"除了可以用来询问方式外，有时还可以用来询问原因，等于"为什么"。

Apart from asking for the manner，"怎么" can also be used to ask for the reason as "why" does.

例如：你今天怎么这样高兴？

6. 你说在哪儿就在哪儿呗！

"……哪儿……哪儿"，两个"哪儿"前后呼应，指同一个地点，它们之间的关系是一种条件关系，也就是说，第一个"哪儿"是第二个"哪儿"的条件，前者决定后者。

In the structure "……哪儿……哪儿"，both "哪儿" refer to the same place while their relationship is conditional，with the first determining the second.

例如：哪儿好玩儿我们就上哪儿玩儿。

7. 带你来看西湖的夜景没白来吧？

"白"，副词，指没有效果，没有达到目的。

"白"，an adverb，means "in vain" or "without success".

例如：这些钱没白花。

185

替换练习　Substitution Drills

1. 杨公堤　　　恢复了　　它原来　　　的　　　模样。
　　这条街　　　　　　　过去　　　　　　　景象
　　那个景点　　　　　　以前　　　　　　　样子
　　这公园　　　　　　　原有　　　　　　　面貌

2. 这里　　　　展示了　　江南水乡　　　的　　　田园风光。
　　他在比赛中　　　　　出众　　　　　　　才能
　　这些照片　　　　　　一片美好　　　　　景象
　　这件事　　　　　　　一个人高尚　　　　品德

3. 这　　　　　是　　　清代　　　　　　　　的　　　杭州城区地形图。
　　那　　　　　　　　　唐代　　　　　　　　　　　彩色雕塑
　　这些图书　　　　　　上个世纪二十年代　　　　　出版物
　　这幅画儿　　　　　　著名画家齐白石　　　　　　代表作品

会话　Conversations

完成下列会话 Complete the following dialogues
（如括号里有词语或提示，请按要求做 Use words or expressions given in the brackets）

　　A：西湖的风景不错吧。
　　B：太美了。
　　A：这一次来西湖游览，值得吧。
　　B：太值得了，＿＿＿＿＿＿＿＿＿＿＿＿＿＿＿＿。（白）

　　A：大牛，今天晚上我请你吃饭？
　　B：太谢谢你了。
　　A：想吃什么呢？
　　B：不用客气，你＿＿＿＿＿＿＿＿＿＿＿＿。（……什么……什么）

杭州

【第十三集】

场景 Scene　西湖御码头

韩　佳：我现在在的地方是西湖边上的御码头。

大　牛：有上船的没有^①? 有上船的没有?

韩　佳：大牛，你怎么跑到这儿来当船夫啦?

大　牛：韩佳，我想跟西湖近距离接触啊! 你知道吗，我可是特意到御码头来接你的呀!

Han Jia: The place I'm at right now is the West Lake's Imperial Dock.

Daniel: Anyone for a boat ride? Anyone?

Han Jia: Daniel, what are you doing here as a boatman?

Daniel: Han Jia, I just wanted to get some close contact with the West Lake. Do you know that I came all the way here just to pick you up?

手划船上

韩　佳：哎，大牛，这儿的风景就挺不错的。你呀也歇一会儿，坐下来欣赏欣赏吧！

大　牛：嗯，好吧！哎，韩佳，我听说改建以后的南线景区也特别好看。要不，今天咱们也过去看看？

韩　佳：行啊，反正船桨在你手中，你划到哪儿我就陪你游到哪儿！

大　牛：好，在西湖上划船，感觉和岸上真是完全不一样！西湖这么美，我大牛怎么着也得作一首诗，赞美一下西湖。

韩　佳：你呀，就别费脑筋了！历史上描写西湖的诗句可多了！哎，最有名的要数苏东坡的那一句。

大　牛：哦，你教教我吧！

韩　佳：听好了啊！"欲把西湖比西子，淡妆浓抹总相宜。"

Yù bǎ Xī Hú bǐ Xīzǐ, dàn zhuāng nóng mǒ zǒng xiāngyí.
欲 把 西 湖 比 西子， 淡 妆 浓 抹 总 相宜。

Just like Xi Shi, the West Lake is beautiful whatever the weather.

大　牛：有一点我不太明白，这"西子"指的是什么呀？

韩　佳："西子"就是指中国古代四大美女之一的西施。苏东坡把西湖比喻成西子，就是说不论淡妆还是浓妆都很好看。

大　牛：这么说，西湖也化妆？

韩　佳：不是，那是指天气。就是说不管风雨阴晴，西湖看上去都那么漂亮②。

大　牛：嗯，一句话，就是说西湖怎么看都好看。

Han Jia: Hey, Daniel, the view here is great. Why don't you take a break and relax for a while.

Daniel: All right. Hey, Han Jia. I heard that the renovated south scenic sites worth a visit. How about going there today?

Han Jia: The oar is in your hands, I'll go wherever you take me.

Daniel: Okay. Rowing on the West Lake feels completely different from standing on the shore. Since the West Lake is so beautiful, I've got to write a poem to praise it.

Han Jia: You don't have to bother, there are countless poems about the West Lake in history. The most famous one is the one by Su Dongpo.

Daniel: Oh, could you teach me, please?

Han Jia: Listen up. Shall I compare thee to Xizi; makeup never hides thy beauty.

Daniel: There's one thing that I don't understand. What does "Xizi" refer to?

Han Jia: "Xizi" refers to one of the four ancient Chinese beauties, Xishi. Su Dongpo compared the West Lake to Xizi, who was beautiful with either light or heavy makeup.

Daniel: The West Lake uses makeup too?

Han Jia: No, he meant the weather. The West Lake is beautiful regardless of the weather conditions.

Daniel: In other words, the West Lake is beautiful at any time.

韩　佳：西湖自古就有"金牛湖"的美称。

大　牛：嗨，你看，我大牛一来，这里就改叫……哎，不对，自古就有。哎，韩佳，你是说它吧？

韩　佳：嗯，没错，这就叫"金牛出水"。相传啊西湖底下有一头金牛，每当湖水要干枯的时候，金牛就会吐水把西湖注满。

Han Jia: Since ancient times, the West Lake was also called the Lake of the Golden Ox.

Daniel: See, as I'm here, the West Lake is now called... since ancient times? Hey, Han Jia, did you say that?

Han Jia: That's right. This is "the Golden Ox Emerging from the Lake". Legend has it that a golden ox lived at the bottom of the West Lake. Whenever the lake was about to dry up, the golden ox would spew out water to fill it up again.

钱王像

韩 佳：大牛你看，这就是钱王像。

大 牛：哇，真威武啊！

韩 佳：嗯，我要考你的这个字啊，就是他名字里的一个字。你看，读什么？

大 牛：钱……这个字啊，我还真不知道念什么！

Zhège zì wǒ hái zhēn bù zhīdao niàn shénme.

这 个 字 我 还 真 不 知 道 念 什 么。

I really don't know what this character reads.

韩 佳：嗯，这个字啊的确挺少见的，恐怕好多中国人也念不准③！

大 牛：那它到底念什么呢？

韩 佳：这个字啊，念"镠（liú）"。

大 牛：哦，"镠（liú）"，第二声，记住喽！

韩 佳：嗯，走！

Han Jia: Look, Daniel. The Qian Wang Statue.

Daniel: Wow, how mighty!

Han Jia: I want to test you on a character in his name. Look, what does it read?

Daniel: Qian... hmm... I really don't know what this character reads.

Han Jia: This is indeed a rare character. Many Chinese don't know what it reads.

Daniel: What does it read anyway?

Han Jia: It actually reads "liu".

Daniel: Ah, "liu". Second tone. I'll remember it.

Han Jia: Let's go.

杭州

场景 Scene　涌金楼

大　牛："涌金楼"，哎，好像是一个吃饭的酒楼。哎哟，韩佳，我的肚子有一点饿！

韩　佳：你不会又想让我请客吧！这"涌金楼"可是南宋时期考取进士和状元之后摆状元宴的地方④。

大　牛：韩佳，我可是中国人民大学的优秀毕业生啊！

韩　佳：据说这状元宴，一般都是状元摆酒席招待别人。

大　牛：啊……韩佳，咱们到那边去看看吧！

韩　佳：哎，你又不饿了？

大　牛：不饿不饿！

Daniel: "Yongjin Lou", looks like it's a restaurant. Han Jia! I'm getting hungry...

Han Jia: Are you trying to make me buy you lunch again? "Yongjin Lou" was a place where who passed the highest imperial exam as the top scholars had banquets.

Daniel: Don't forget that I'm an excellent graduate of Renmin University of China.

Han Jia: I heard that the Number One scholar paid for the banquet.

Daniel: Uh... Let's go over there...

Han Jia: Hey, I thought you were hungry!

Daniel: No, no...

学士桥

大　牛：韩佳，这几天游西湖啊，我们过了各式各样不同造型的桥，你看，这里又是一座小桥。

韩　佳：这座是近两年刚修复的学士桥。

大　牛：学士桥？那是不是那边有硕士桥、博士桥⑤？

韩　佳：这"学士"是对苏东坡的尊称。这位杭州市的老市长，建苏堤、造六桥、立三塔，功不可没啊！

大　牛："功不可没"？这又是一个成语吧？

韩　佳：对呀，"功不可没"呢是指他们的功绩永远不能磨灭。

大　牛：哦，我知道了。"功不可没"是一个成语，是指他们的功绩永远不能磨灭。

gōng bù kě mò

功 不 可 没

undeniable merits and virtues

Daniel: Han Jia, We've seen bridges of different styles at the West Lake in the past few days. Look, there's another one.

Han Jia: This is Xueshi Bridge, renovated a few years ago.

Daniel: Xueshi Bridge? Bachelor Bridge? Is there also a Master or a Doctor Bridge?

Han Jia: "Xueshi" is a honorary title for Su Dongpo. This former mayor of Hangzhou constructed one causeway, six bridges, and three pagodas. "Gong bu ke mo".

Daniel: Is "gong bu ke mo" another idiom?

Han Jia: That's right. "Gong bu ke mo" means that someone's achievements will never be forgotten.

Daniel: I see. "Gong bu ke mo" is a Chinese idiom, which means that someone's achievements will never be forgotten.

大　牛：哎，韩佳，看来现代杭州人为了让西湖变得更加美丽，还真
　　　　做了不少呢！

韩　佳：是啊，每个人都在为西湖做出自己的贡献，这样才能吸引更
　　　　多的朋友来游西湖、逛杭州。哎，这几天正好是西湖博览会
　　　　召开的日子⑥，晚上我带你去看礼花。

大　牛：太好了！西湖上放礼花，那得多美呀！

韩　佳：我们的口号是：学说中国话，朋友遍天下！

大　牛：跟着我们俩一起看礼花，走！

Daniel: Hey, Han Jia. It seems that people of Hangzhou today have done quite a lot to improve the West Lake.

Han Jia: That's right. Everybody is making his own contribution to the West Lake. This is the way to attract more friends to come and visit Hangzhou. The West Lake Exposition is going on right now. I'll take you to see fireworks tonight.

Daniel: Great! Fireworks over the West Lake. Sounds fantastic!

Han Jia: Our motto is: Chinese learned, friends earned!

Daniel: Fireworks, here we come!

生词 Words and Expressions

1.	码头	（名）	mǎtou	dock
2.	特意	（副）	tèyì	especially
3.	划船		huá chuán	boating
4.	诗	（名）	shī	poem
5.	不管	（连）	bùguǎn	no matter what/how
6.	恐怕	（副）	kǒngpà	I'm afraid...
7.	优秀	（形）	yōuxiù	outstanding
8.	吸引	（动）	xīyǐn	to attract
9.	博览会	（名）	bólǎnhuì	fair, exhibition

注释 Notes

1. 有上船的没有？

这是用"有"和"没有"组成的正反问句，宾语可以放在"有"的后边，也可以放在"没有"的后边。本句也可以说成"有没有上船的？"

This is a positive-negative question formed by "有" and "没有". The object can be put after "有" or "没有". The structure means "Is there anyone who...?" or "Anyone who...?". "有没有上船的" can also be used instead of "有上船的没有".

例如：有没有去西湖的？

2. 就是说不管风雨阴晴，西湖看上去都那么漂亮。

这是个条件复句。"不管……都（也）……"表示在任何条件或情况下，结果都不会改变。

"不管……都（也）……", a conditional complex sentence, is equivalent to "no matter what/how..." in English.

例如：明天的活动，不管谁来参加我们都欢迎。

3. 恐怕好多中国人也念不准！

"恐怕"，副词，表示估计并担心。

"恐怕", an adverb in Chinese, means "I'm afraid..."

例如：如果你一定要这样做，恐怕效果不会好。

4. 这"涌金楼"可是南宋时期考取进士和状元之后摆状元宴的地方。

从隋唐到清朝，封建王朝考选官吏后备人员，凡参加皇帝亲自主持的最高一级考试并考取的人称为进士，第一名称为状元。

From the Sui and Tang Dynasties to the Qing Dynasty, when feudal courts selected officials, those who passed the highest-level examination presided over by the emperor were called "进士", and among them, the one who came first was called "状元".

5. 那是不是那边有硕士桥、博士桥？

汉语里，有一种用"是不是"的正反问句，如果提问的人对某一事物或情况有比较肯定的估计，为了进一步证实，常用这种问句。"是不是"可以放在陈述句的谓语前，也可以放在句子的开头或结尾。

"是不是" is used to confirm an answer to a question, and it can be put before the predicate, or at the beginning or end of a sentence as a question tag.

例如：那边是不是有银行？

那边是不是有银行？

那边有银行是不是？

"是不是"有时也可以用来征求对方的意见，这时候"是不是"不能放在句子后面。

Also, sometimes it can be used when asking for the other's opinion, and in this case, "是不是" cannot be put at the end.

例如：我们是不是给他打个电话？

是不是我们给他打个电话？

6. 这几天正好是西湖博览会召开的日子……

"正好"，副词，这里表示时间不前不后，恰好。这句话的意思是"恰好西湖博览会正在召开"。

"正好", an adverb, meaning "right". And the sentence means "Right now, the West Lake Exposition is going on".

例如：你来得正好，我刚要给你打电话。

替换练习　Substitution Drills

这个	字	我还真不知道	念	什么。
	人		叫	
	工厂		生产	
	电影院		演	

会话　Conversations

完成下列会话 Complete the following dialogues
（如括号里有词语或提示，请按要求做 Use words or expressions given in the brackets）

A：明天去逛公园吗？
B：去。
A：要是天气不好呢？
B：＿＿＿＿＿＿＿＿＿＿＿＿＿＿＿。（不管……都……）

● ●

A：这个字怎么念？
B：不知道，这个字很少见。
A：问问林克吧。
B：＿＿＿＿＿＿＿＿＿＿＿＿＿＿＿。（恐怕）

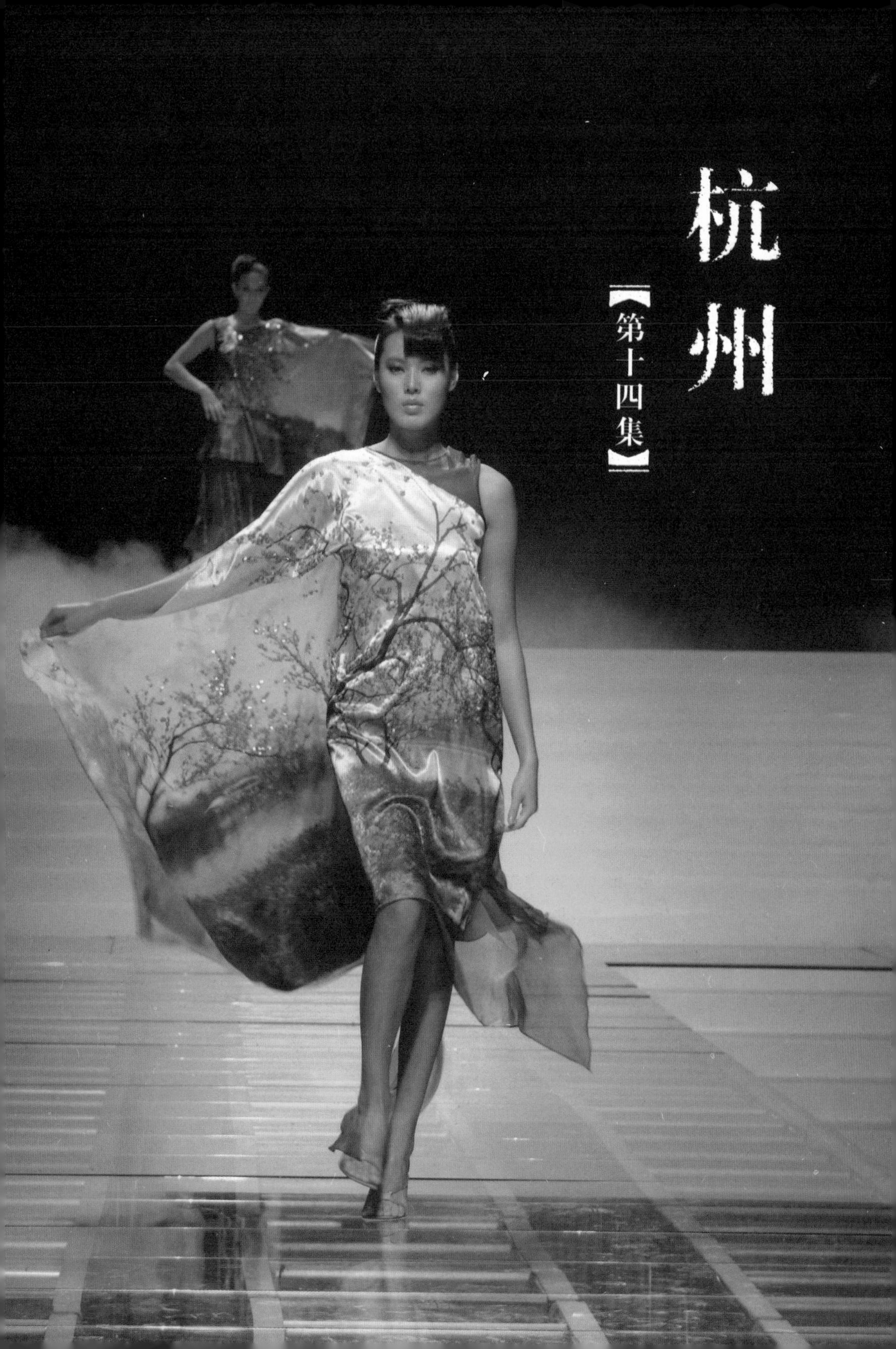
杭州
【第十四集】

韩　佳：大家好！快乐的韩佳在《快乐中国》向您问好！这几天，新丝路模特大赛正在杭州举行。你们看这些模特们穿着"西湖十景"的衣服，多漂亮啊！今天大牛没来可亏了！

大　牛：快乐学汉语，轻松又好记！快乐的大牛在这儿呢！

韩　佳：大牛，人家都在展示西湖美景，你跑这儿捣什么乱啊①！

大　牛：我呀，也是西湖一景。

韩　佳：西湖新老二十景，你算哪一景啊！

大　牛：这二十景里肯定没有我。不过，我们不是最近去过涌金门吗？我这是"金牛出水"。

韩　佳：亏你想得出来，快下去吧②！大家还要看服装表演呢！

大　牛：哦，好！

Dàjiā　hái　yào　kàn　fúzhuāng　biǎoyǎn　ne!
大家　还　要　看　服装　表演　呢!

People are waiting to watch the fashion show.

Han Jia: Hello, everybody. Happy Han Jia says hello from Happy China. The New Silk Road Fashion Contest is going on in Hangzhou these days. These models are wearing clothes depicting the ten scenes of the West Lake. Aren't they gorgeous? What a pity that Daniel's not here today!

Daniel: Learning Chinese with joy and ease! Happy Daniel is right here!

Han Jia: They're showing the views of the West Lake, What are you doing here?

Daniel: Well, I'm one of the scenes!

Han Jia: here are 20 scenes of the West Lake. Which one are you?

Daniel: Well, I'm not one of those 20. However, remember Yongjinmen? I'm the "Golden Ox Emerging from the Lake".

Han Jia: Yeah, yeah... Hurry up and get off the stage. People are waiting to see the fashion show.

Daniel: All right.

杭州

杭州街景

大　牛：韩佳，你看我这件衣服怎么样？他们说是正宗的杭州丝绸。

韩　佳：你还挺会挑！中国的丝绸有着悠久的历史，世界闻名。

大　牛：嗯，没错！

韩　佳：哎，既然你对丝绸这么感兴趣，我带你到中国丝绸博物馆去看看？

大　牛：太好了，走吧！

陈　琴：哎，韩佳！

韩　佳：哎，琴琴你好！我给你介绍一下，这位是我的朋友陈琴，这位是我的搭档大牛。

陈　琴：大牛，你好！

大　牛：陈琴，你好！刚才看了你们在舞台上的表演，感觉真棒！

陈　琴：谢谢！

大　牛：下次演出的时候，一定要把我叫过来！

陈　琴：没问题！哎，韩佳，你们先忙吧，我先走了。对了，别忘了下午的活动！再见！

韩　佳：放心吧，忘不了，下午见！

大　牛：韩佳，你下午有什么活动啊？

韩　佳：哦，没什么……走，我们到丝绸博物馆去吧！

Daniel: What do you think about my shirt, Han Jia? They tell me it's made of authentic Hangzhou silk.

Han Jia: Nice pick, indeed. Chinese silk has a long history and is known throughout the world.

Daniel: That's right.

Han Jia: Since you're so interested in silk, why not go to the China Silk Museum with me?

Daniel: That'd be great!

Chen Qin: Hey, Han Jia!

Han Jia: Hey, Qinqin! Let me make an introduction. This is my friend, Chen Qin. And this is my partner, Daniel.

Chen Qin: Hello, Daniel.

Daniel: Hi, Chen Qin. I just saw your performance on stage. It was wonderful!

Chen Qin: Thank you!

Daniel: Don't forget to let me know the next time you have a show.

Chen Qin: No problem! Hey, Han Jia, I'm going to let you guys get back to work. Don't forget the arrangement of this afternoon! See you later!

Han Jia: Don't worry, I won't. See you!

Daniel: Han Jia, what's your plan for this afternoon?

Han Jia: Um, nothing... Let's get going to the silk museum.

丝绸博物馆大厅

大　牛：原来我的衣服是这样织出来的呀！

韩　佳：哪有那么简单！要得到一块好的丝绸啊，先得养蚕，再取丝，然后纺织等等等等③。复杂着呢！

大　牛：哎，韩佳，我想试两下。

韩　佳：你行吗？

大　牛：没事儿，有师傅指导呢。

韩　佳：完了！这快丝绸算是卖不出去了④。

zhè kuài sīchóu suànshì mài bù chūqù le.
这 块 丝绸 算是 卖 不 出去 了。

They won't be able to sell this piece of silk anymore.

Daniel: So this is how my shirt was made!

Han Jia: It's not that simple. In order to produce a nice piece of silk, you have to first raise silkworms, then extract the silk threads, and then do the weaving... It's very complicated.

Daniel: Hey, Han Jia. I want to give it a try.

Han Jia: You?

Daniel: Don't worry, we've got a master worker here.

Han Jia: My Gosh, this piece of silk won't get sold any more.

　丝绸展柜

大　牛：“绿草百蝶暗花缎底五彩绣”。天哪，这件衣服的名字和它的制作工艺一样复杂呀⑤！哎，韩佳，形容技艺精巧，用什么词比较合适啊？

韩　佳：教你一个词吧，“精湛”，我们通常说“精湛的技艺”。“精湛”就是精深的意思，是指精密深奥。

大　牛：哦，“精湛”就是精细。韩佳，这件衣服的做工的确很精湛，佩服！哎，韩佳，那就是皇帝穿的龙袍吧？

韩　佳：嗯，那可是乾隆皇帝穿过的！走，我们过去看看！

大　牛：嗯，皇帝就是皇帝⑥！你们看，他穿的衣服都是金光闪闪的！

韩　佳：大牛，你看旁边的那套盔甲，那是清代的军人穿的。

大　牛：嗯，不错！

韩　佳：哎呀，忘了，我还约了陈琴呢！快来不及了！哎，大牛，你先自己慢慢看，我要走了！

大　牛：哎，韩佳，等等，你和她约好要去干什么呀？

韩　佳：我和她约好要去丝绸城买丝绸。

Wǒ hé tā yuēhǎo qù mǎi sīchóu.
我 和 她 约好 去 买 丝绸。

We arranged to go silk shopping together.

Daniel: "Lü cao bai die an hua duan di wu cai xiu"? My goodness, the name of this piece of garment is as complicated as the craft used to make it. Han Jia, what's the good word for describing a refined craft?

Han Jia: Let me tell you a word: "jingzhan". We would normally say a craft is "jingzhan". "Jingzhan" means exquisite, refined and profound.

Daniel: "Jingzhan" means intricate. Han Jia, the craft of this piece of garment is very "jingzhan". Very impressive! Hey, Han Jia, is that an imperial robe?

Han Jia: Yep. That very one was worn by the Emperor Qianlong. Let's go and take a look.

Daniel: Wow, it's imperial indeed. Look, the emperor's robe is glowing with gold.

Han Jia: See the set of armor next to you, Daniel? That was used by the soldiers of the Qing Dynasty.

Daniel: Not bad...

Han Jia: Oh, I almost forgot. I have to meet Chen Qin! It's almost the time! Take your time here, Daniel. I need to get going.

Daniel: Hey, wait, Han Jia. What did you guys plan to do?

Han Jia: We've arranged to go shopping for silk.

场景 Scene 丝绸馆外

大　牛：她们两个女孩子购物去了，也不带我去。反正在湖边喝酒也不错。

韩　佳：大牛，我回来了！你看，好看吗？刚买的。

大　牛：好看！

韩　佳：还有这件，怎么样？

大　牛：好看！

韩　佳：你怎么都不看啊？

大　牛：还是你们女孩子好，又能买丝巾，又能买什么旗袍⑦。

韩　佳：哎，生闷气哪？我给你也买了礼物啦。

大　牛：啊？给我买了一件礼物啊？哎呀，韩佳，你太客气啦！给我看一下吧！

韩　佳：是一件衣服！

大　牛：这是给我买的啊？

韩　佳：给它呀！

大　牛：哦，原来是瓶套，做得还挺精致啊！

Daniel: The girls went shopping and wouldn't take me along. Having some quiet wine by the lake isn't so bad...

Han Jia: I'm back, Daniel! Look, isn't this pretty? I just bought it.

Daniel: Yeah...

Han Jia: What about this one?

Daniel: Yeah...

Han Jia: You're not even looking!

Daniel: It's lucky to be a girl. You can just go out and buy scarves, cheong-sam...

Han Jia: Why, are you upset? I bought something for you too.

Daniel: Really? A gift for me? You're very kind, Han Jia. Can I see it?

Han Jia: It's a piece of clothes.

Daniel: Huh? Is this for me?

Han Jia: It's for that!

Daniel: Ah, it's a bottle cover. Very elegant!

生词　Words and Expressions

1. 模特　　（名）　　mótè　　　　model
2. 捣乱　　　　　　　dǎo luàn　　to make trouble
3. 服装　　（名）　　fúzhuāng　　clothing
4. 表演　　（动）　　biǎoyǎn　　to perform
5. 丝绸　　（名）　　sīchóu　　　silk
6. 技艺　　（名）　　jìyì　　　　skill
7. 精湛　　（形）　　jīngzhàn　　exquisite
8. 佩服　　（动）　　pèifú　　　to admire
9. 约　　　（动）　　yuē　　　　to make an appointment

注释　Notes

1. 你跑这儿捣什么乱啊!

　　"捣什么乱"，"捣乱"中间加"什么"表示不满意、厌烦。

　　"什么" is added in between "捣乱" to show the speaker's dissatisfaction or annoyance.

　　例如：我们正忙呢，你来这儿捣什么乱!

2. 亏你想得出来，快下去吧!

　　"亏"，动词，表示对事情不满、轻视或讽刺。

　　"亏"，a verb, is used to show the speaker's dissatisfaction, scorn or irony.

　　例如：这样的话亏你说得出口。

3. 要得到一块好的丝绸啊，先得养蚕，再取丝，然后纺织等等等等。

　　"先……再……然后……"这一结构表示几个动作相继出现的次序。

　　"先……再……然后……"，the structure is used to introduce the sequence of a series of actions.

　　例如：这是一件大事，大家要先做好准备再进行讨论，然后做出决定。

　　"等"和"等等"都是助词，表示列举未尽，可以叠用，用在两个或两个以上并列的词语后面。

"等" or "等等" are auxiliary words similar to "and so on", "etc." in English.

例如：桌子上摆满了报纸、杂志、书本、词典等等。

4. 这块丝绸算是卖不出去了。

"算是"，副词，可以用来表示推测肯定会出现某种结果。

"算是"，an adverb, can be used to affirm a certain result.

例如：这一次算是大功告成了。

5. 这件衣服的名字和它的制作工艺一样复杂呀！

"和（跟）……一样"这一结构用于比较两个人或两种事物性状的异同，在句子中可以做谓语，也可以做定语或状语。

The structure "和（跟）……一样" is used to compare two persons or things. It can be used as the predicate, attribute or adverbial.

例如：我的自行车和他的自行车一样。（谓语）

他也想买一件和这一件一样的礼物。（定语）

这件衣服的名字和它的制作工艺一样复杂。（状语）

6. 皇帝就是皇帝！

"A 就是 A"这一结构，这里用来强调事物的客观性。

"A 就是 A" is used to emphasize the objectivity of things.

"皇帝就是皇帝"这句话的意思是：皇帝跟老百姓的确不一样，皇帝穿的衣服都是金光闪闪的，跟老百姓穿的不一样。

The meaning of the sentence is like this: The emperor is not like common citizens, he wears glittering clothes.

例如：事实就是事实，你想不承认也不行。

7. 还是你们女孩子好，又能买丝巾，又能买什么旗袍。

"还是"，副词，这里表示经过比较、考虑后的选择。

"还是"，an adverb, is used to indicate that a choice is made after deliberation.

例如：还是坐飞机去吧，坐火车太慢了。

替换练习　Substitution Drills

1. | 大家 | 还要看 | 服装表演 | 呢！ |
他们		篮球比赛	
我们		书法展览	
大牛		画展	

2. | 这块丝绸 | 算是 | 卖不出去 | 了。 |
这些作业		做不完	
这件事		我倒霉	
这架飞机		晚点	

3. | 我和她 | 约好去 | 买丝绸。 |
我们		看电影
大家		登长城
我和朋友		游西湖

会话　Conversations

完成下列会话 Complete the following dialogues
（如括号里有词语或提示，请按要求做 Use words or expressions given in the brackets）

A：我想买一件旗袍，你帮我挑一挑吧。
B：你喜欢什么颜色的？
A：_____。（还是）
B：我也喜欢红色的，那就买这一件吧。

A：听说你去过中国好多城市，是吗？
B：是啊。
A：这两年都去过哪些城市呢？
B：_____。（等等）

218

杭州

【第十五集】

宋城城楼前

大　牛：哎，韩佳，你看，这里有这么多古代建筑。这是什么地方啊？

韩　佳：新鲜吧①？这里就是著名的宋城。哎，我可告诉你，进到这里来的人啊，都要像中国宋朝时候的人那么说话、那么生活。

大　牛：啊，原来是这样！那你得好好教教我，这宋朝的人是怎么说话呀？

Daniel: Hey, Han Jia, look, there are so many ancient structures here. Where are we?

Han Jia: Is it interesting? It is the famous Song Cheng. Hey, I would like to remind you that people who come here will have to talk and live like people in the Song Dynasty did.

Daniel: Wow, I see. You must teach me how people in the Song Dynasty spoke.

城楼下

大　牛：哎，韩佳，我这样走像不像宋代人啊？

韩　佳：嗯，有那么点意思，还不错！

大　牛：那是！

韩　佳：这个大牛！

大　牛：哦，不，韩佳，你过奖了，过奖过奖！

韩　佳：瞧瞧，大牛也谦虚起来了，这可是破天荒头一次啊！

Tā yě qiānxū qilai le, zhè kě shì pòtiānhuāng tóu yí cì a!
他 也 谦虚 起来 了，这 可是 破天荒 头 一 次 啊！

All of sudden he's modest. Well, that certainly is a first.

大　牛：什么？我"破天荒"？

韩　佳："破天荒"是一个惯用语，"天荒"是指没有开垦的土地，"开垦荒地"就是比喻事情的第一次。

大　牛：哦，原来如此啊！

Daniel: Hey, Han Jia. Do I walk like people in the Song Dynasty did?

Han Jia: Well, a little, not bad.

Daniel: Of course.

Han Jia: Daniel.

Daniel: Oh, well, I am flattered.

Han Jia: See, Daniel becomes modest too. It has never happened before.

Daniel: What? "Potianhuang"?

Han Jia: "Potianhuang" is a phrase. "Tianhuang" refers to virgin land. Cultivating plants on virgin land is a metaphor of doing something for the first fime.

Daniel: Oh, I see.

韩　佳：牛公子，你远来是客，说说想看点儿什么吧②！

大　牛：哎呀，太多了！哎哟，这是干吗呀？马队都出来了！

韩　佳：大牛，不，牛公子，这是巡城的马队，你看那些小伙子们的骑术，很不错吧！

大　牛：嗯，我觉得我已经骑得不错，没想到中国古代的骑士，装扮起来更威风。

韩　佳：这叫"人外有人，天外有天"③嘛。

Rén wài yǒu rén, tiān wài yǒu tiān.

人 外 有 人，天 外 有 天。

There is no limit to learning or skills.

Han Jia: Mr. Daniel, you are a guest from far away. What would you like to see?

Daniel: Well, lots of things. What are they doing? The cavalry comes out.

Han Jia: Daniel. I mean, Mr. Daniel, this is the cavalry for city patrol. Do you think the guys are good at horseback riding?

Daniel: Yes. I thought I am a good horseback rider. I didn't expect that ancient Chinese cavaliers were more dignified in uniform.

Han Jia: There are wiser people and vaster space out there.

草编摊

韩 佳：哎，大牛，你看，这些草编的小动物多形象啊！

大 牛：嗯，用我们学过的一句成语，就是"栩栩如生"。

韩 佳：嗯，没错，大牛你还不选一个！

大 牛：好，那我就买一头"牛"吧！

韩 佳：嗯，这头牛编得还真像！

大 牛：师傅，给您钱！

师 傅：客官！找你钱！

大 牛：不用了，不用了，谢谢！

韩 佳：哎，大牛，今天你怎么这么大方啊④？

Jīntiān nǐ zénme zhème dàfang a?
今天 你 怎么 这么 大方 啊？

Why are you so generous today?

韩 佳：今天你怎么这么大方啊？连找钱都不要了。

大 牛：我呀，高兴！我大牛长这么大从来没做过官，但是今天我终于当官了。

韩 佳：啊，什么时候啊？

大 牛：就刚才嘛！你没听见他叫我什么官？反正是官！

韩 佳：客官吧！

大 牛：哦，对对对！哎，韩佳，"客官"这个官大不大呀？

韩 佳：反正古代人管顾客都叫"客官"⑤。

大 牛：啊？不是官啊！

Han Jia: Hey, Daniel, look, the straw-woven animals are so vivid.

Daniel: Right. To describe them with an idiom we learned, it is "xuxu ru sheng".

Han Jia: Right, Daniel. Why don't you pick one?

Daniel: All right. I will buy a bull.

Han Jia: Yes, the bull is so vivid.

Daniel: Here you are, Master.

Craftman: Here is your change, "keguan".

Daniel: Keep it please. Thank you.

Han Jia: Hey, Daniel, why are you so generous today? You didn't even accept your change.

Daniel: I am so happy. I have never been an officer before, but today I finally became one.

Han Jia: Well, when?

Daniel: Just now, didn't you hear he called me some kind of "guan"?

Han Jia: "Keguan".

Daniel: Right. Hey, Han Jia, is "keguan" a high or low rank?

Han Jia: Ancient people called all customers "keguan".

Daniel: So it is not an officer?

宋城糖画摊

卖糖者：看一下，糖块糖块啦！又好吃又好看，糖块糖块！

大　牛：韩佳，你看，糖块，糖块。没想到古时候就已经有我大牛爱吃的这种美食！

韩　佳：牛公子！

大　牛：对，我牛公子对吃的不感兴趣。咱们还是去看看诗词、书画吧！

韩　佳：哎，这儿啊，还真有书画呢！

手指画

大　牛：哎，韩佳，我没看错吧！他画画儿好像用的就是手指头啊！

画画者：哎，对呀！这就是特殊的艺术——手指画。

群　众：快去看看！

大　牛：哎，刚才那几个人干吗去了？

画画者：哎，客官，你们还不知道吗？这里王员外家小姐抛绣球呢⑥。你们还是过去看一下！

韩　佳：抛绣球！大牛，今天咱们可赶上喜事了！

大　牛：哎，抛绣球是什么球啊？怎么玩啊！

韩　佳：赶紧过去看看！

画画者：哎，客官，你的画儿还没拿去呢！

Candy vendor: Look, candy, candy. Sweet and nice candy.

Daniel: Han Jia, look, candy. I didn't expect that there was my favorite candy in ancient times.

Han Jia: Mr. Daniel.

Daniel: Right. I am not interested in food. Let's go to see the poems, verses, calligraphy and paintings.

Han Jia: Well, there are calligraphy and paintings here indeed.

Daniel: Hey, Han Jia, am I seeing this right? He's using his fingers to paint.

Painter: Right. This is the special artistic finger painting.

People: Go over quickly and check it out.

Daniel: Hey, where did those guys go?

Painter: Hey, sir, don't you know that the daughter of counsellor Wang is throwing the embroidered ball? You'd better go and check it out.

Han Jia: "Pao xiuqiu". Daniel, we are lucky to catch this happy event.

Daniel: Hey, what is "pao xiuqiu"? How do you play it?

Han Jia: Hey, go over quickly and take a look.

Painter: Hey, "keguan", you forgot to take your painting.

王员外家楼下

大　牛：哎，各位让一让，让一下！

韩　佳：哎，牛公子，现在可到你表现的时候了，你要是能够抢到绣球，
　　　　得到王家小姐的青睐，那可真是为我们《快乐中国》争光了！

大　牛：什么什么？她的青……

韩　佳：快快快！开始了，开始了！

群　众：哎，给我给我，来来来！

大　牛：我抢到球了！

韩　佳：大牛，你真棒！

大　牛：哎，真是喜从天降！那接下来会不会发奖啊？

韩　佳：接下来这个，我们先来看"赏心悦目"，一会儿我再悄悄告
　　　　诉你。

大　牛：好，一起喊出我们《快乐中国》的口号！

　合：学说中国话，朋友遍天下！

韩　佳：要想知道牛公子的结局呀，咱们明天节目中再见！

Daniel: Hey, excuse me, excuse me.

Han Jia: Hey, Mr. Daniel, it's time for you to show your competence. If you can catch the embroidered ball and win the favor of Miss Wang, you will bring honor to Happy China.

Daniel: What? What did you say?

Han Jia: It's starting.

People: Hey, Miss Wang, throw it to me.

Daniel: I got the ball!

Han Jia: Daniel, you are fabulous!

Daniel: Hey, I am really lucky today. Are they going to present me with a prize?

Han Jia: Next let's go to the Feast for the Eyes first. I will tell you later in secret.

Daniel: OK. Please say the motto of Happy China together.

All: Chinese learned, friends earned!

Han Jia: If you want to know what is going on with Mr. Daniel, please tune in to our program tomorrow.

生词　Words and Expressions

1. 谦虚	（形）	qiānxū	modest
2. 惯用语	（名）	guànyòngyǔ	idiom
3. 装扮	（动）	zhuāngbàn	to dress up
4. 威风	（形）	wēifēng	majestic looking
5. 大方	（形）	dàfang	generous
6. 顾客	（名）	gùkè	customer
7. 抛	（动）	pāo	to throw
8. 绣球	（名）	xiùqiú	embroidered ball
9. 悄悄	（副）	qiāoqiāo	quietly

注释　Notes

1. 新鲜吧？

"新鲜"这里是"稀罕少见"的意思。

"新鲜" does not mean "fresh" here, and it means "rare" instead.

例如：会用计算机，这已经不算是什么新鲜事了。

2. 说说想看点儿什么吧！

"点儿"，表示少量。

"点儿" means "a bit", "a small quantity".

例如：你想喝点儿什么？

3. 人外有人，天外有天。

这句话经常用来表示学问、技术、本领等是没有止境的。

The saying is often used to mean that there is no limit to learning.

例如：你汉语说得确实不错，但是人外有人，天外有天，所以你还应该继续努力，不要骄傲。

4. 今天你怎么这么大方啊？

"这么"，代词，这里表示程度，含有和以前比较的意思。"你今天怎么这么大方”意思是“以前你从来没有今天这样大方”。

“这么”，a pronoun indicating degree，is used to implicate comparison with previous situation. The meaning implied here is "you have never been so generous before".

例如：你今天来得这么早！

5. 反正古代人管顾客都叫“客官”。

“管……叫……”这一结构用来指称人或事情，只用于口语。

“管……叫……”，an oral expression，is used to mean "to call".

例如：因为他姓赵，年纪又比较大，所以大家管他叫老赵。

6. 这里王员外家小姐抛绣球呢。

“呢”，助词，用在陈述句句尾，表示动作正在进行，常和“正”、“正在”、“在”等词搭配。

“呢”，an auxiliary word，put at the end of a declarative sentence means an action is going on. It is often used with “正”，“正在” or “在”.

例如：同学们正上课呢。

服务员在聊天呢。

代表们正在开会呢。

有关“动作正在进行”请参见本书第五集注②。

As for“动作正在进行”，please refer to Note 2，Lesson 5 of this volume.

替换练习　Substitution Drills

1. 你也　　谦虚起来　　　　了，这可是破天荒头一次啊！
　　　　　来跳舞
　　　　　自己洗衣服
　　　　　得奖

· ·

2. 今天，你怎么这么　　大方　　　啊？
　　　　　　　　　　高兴
　　　　　　　　　　谦虚
　　　　　　　　　　别扭

会话　Conversations

完成下列会话 Complete the following dialogues
（如括号里有词语或提示，请按要求做 Use words or expressions given in the brackets）

A：那个亭子挺有意思的，我们去看看吧。
B：那个亭子有几个角？
A：八个，所以人们 _____。（管……叫……）
B：八角亭，名字好听。

· ·

A：张明在吗？
B：在。
A：他在干什么？
B：_____。（呢）

城市风情

杭州，是中国的历史文化名城，历来以风景秀丽著称于世，素有"人间天堂"之誉。

最宜人的季节

杭州四季分明，年平均气温16.2℃，春季(3～5月)和秋季(9～11月)冷暖适中，为最佳旅游季节。

必游景点

苏堤春晓	曲院风荷	平湖秋月	柳浪闻莺	花港观鱼
雷峰夕照	南屏晚钟	三潭印月	虎跑梦泉	龙井问茶

风味特产/地方美食

杭州特产有龙井茶、西湖绸伞、王星记扇子；

传统名菜有东坡肉、西湖醋鱼、叫花童鸡、龙井虾仁、荷叶粉蒸肉等；

著名小吃有葱包桧、虾爆鳝面、知味小笼、猫耳朵等。

与外交通

目前杭州已开通空中航线40多条，从杭州萧山国际机场乘飞机可直达东京、大阪、首尔、釜山、曼谷、新加坡、北京、香港、澳门、上海、广州等30多个大中城市和地区。从杭州乘火车可达北京、上海、天津、重庆、广州、西安、南京、桂林等城市。杭州公路四通八达，快速便捷；京杭运河与钱塘江两条水路航线舒适休闲。

特别提示

每年的10月15日～30日举行杭州西湖博览会，是杭州百姓和中外游客的节日。

钱江潮是世界奇观，农历每月初一至初五、十六至二十都有大潮可观，尤其以农历八月十八前后潮势最大。

畅游杭州 温馨提示

图书在版编目（CIP）数据

快乐中国——学汉语. 杭州篇 /《快乐中国——学汉语》栏目组编.
—北京：北京语言大学出版社，2009 重印
ISBN 978 - 7 - 5619 - 1588 - 2

Ⅰ. 快…

Ⅱ. 快…

Ⅲ. 汉语 - 视听教学 - 对外汉语教学 - 教材

Ⅳ. H195.4

中国版本图书馆 CIP 数据核字（2006）第 012952 号

书　　　名：	快乐中国——学汉语. 杭州篇	
责任编辑：	于　晶	
整体设计：	张志伟　贾　英	
责任印制：	汪学发	

出版发行：**北京语言大学出版社**

社　　　址：北京市海淀区学院路 15 号　邮政编码：100083
网　　　址：www.blcup.com
电　　　话：发行部　82303650 / 3591 / 3651
　　　　　　编辑部　82303647
　　　　　　读者服务部　82303653 / 3908
　　　　　　网上订购电话　82303668
　　　　　　客户服务信箱　service@blcup.net
印　　　刷：北京中科印刷有限公司
经　　　销：全国新华书店

版　　　次：2007 年 4 月第 1 版　2009 年 4 月第 2 次印刷
开　　　本：710 毫米×980 毫米　1/16　印张：15.25
字　　　数：236 千字　　印数：4001 - 7000 册
书　　　号：ISBN 978 - 7 - 5619 - 1588 - 2 / H·06015
定　　　价：79.00 元

凡有印装质量问题，本社负责调换。电话：82303590